A Text Book on Welding and Cutting Metals

Vulcan Process Co, Charles Herbert Burrows

Copyright © BiblioLife, LLC

BiblioLife Reproduction Series: Our goal at BiblioLife is to help readers, educators and researchers by bringing back in print hard-to-find original publications at a reasonable price and, at the same time, preserve the legacy of literary history. The following book represents an authentic reproduction of the text as printed by the original publisher and may contain prior copyright references. While we have attempted to accurately maintain the integrity of the original work(s), from time to time there are problems with the original book scan that may result in minor errors in the reproduction, including imperfections such as missing and blurred pages, poor pictures, markings and other reproduction issues beyond our control. Because this work is culturally important, we have made it available as a part of our commitment to protecting, preserving and promoting the world's literature.

All of our books are in the "public domain" and some are derived from Open Source projects dedicated to digitizing historic literature. We believe that when we undertake the difficult task of re-creating them as attractive, readable and affordable books, we further the mutual goal of sharing these works with a larger audience. A portion of BiblioLife profits go back to Open Source projects in the form of a donation to the groups that do this important work around the world. If you would like to make a donation to these worthy Open Source projects, or would just like to get more information about these important initiatives, please visit www.bibliolife.com/opensource.

A TEXT BOOK

ON

WELDING AND CUTTING METALS

BY THE

Oxyacetylene Process

WITH SIXTY-FOUR ILLUSTRATIONS

THIRD EDITION—REVISED

Copyrighted 1915
By C. H. BURROWS

VULCAN PROCESS CO.
MINNEAPOLIS, MINN.

PREFACE TO THIRD EDITION

It is only a short time since the second edition was issued, and it is gratifying to find that the supply is nearly exhaused There are many mechanics and autogenous welders who desire short, clear and practical instructions on the subject of oxyacetylene welding and it is the purpose of this book to fill this demand

A comprehensive treatise on this subject would necessarily include much technical material that would be useless to the practical man who wishes to acquaint himself with only enough theory to thoroughly master the performance of his duties, and for this reason we have excluded nearly everything of a strictly technical nature.

The Chapters on chemistry, physics and metals are of the most elementary nature, and cover in the plainest language only the subjects that are vital to the welders information. At the same time they are sufficiently explicit to give him a thorough working knowledge of the subjects that pertain to his work

In compiling these pages we have consulted the works on the Manufacture and Properties of Iron and Steel, By H. H. Campbell. The Metallurgy of Iron and Steel, by Bradley Stoughton, and Autogenous Welding, By Granzon and Rosemberg; and some of the text relating to generators and welding has been condensed from papers which we contributed to a few of the leading magazines.

C. H. Burrows

CONTENTS

Story of Vulcan, (Mythology)	VII
Chapter 1. The use of the oxy-acetylene flame	4
Chapter 2. Chemistry	11

    The Elements, Table of Chemical Symbols, and Atomic Weights, Chemical Affinity, The Atomic Theory, Valence, Reaction, Combustion, Flame, Oxygen, Hydrogen, Nitrogen, Calcium Carbide, Acetylene

Chapter 3 Physics	25

    Pneumatics, Boyles Law, Heat, The Calorie, The British Thermal Unit, Temperature, Centigrade and Fahrenheit, Table comparing degrees Centigrade and Fahrenheit, Expansion, Table of Coefficients of Expansion with instructions on its use.

Chapter 4 Metals and their Properties	35

    The Ferrous Group, Cast Iron, Malleable Iron, Wrought Iron, Steel, The Blister Process, Copper, Brass, Aluminum, Alloys.

Chapter 5 Acetylene Generators	44

    Drip Type, Flooding Type, Carbide to Water Type, Selecting A Generator.

Chapter 6 Oxy-Acetylene Welding and Cutting Torches	50

    Low Pressure, High Pressure, Cutting Torches

Chapter 7. Regulators and Indicators	58

    Their manipulation

Chapter 8. The Vulcan Automatic Acetylene Generator	61

    Its operation and manipulation

Chapter 9. Operating Plants

    Compressed Gas Plants, Generator Plants, Pipe installation

Chapter 10 Welding Rods and Fluxes	68

    The theory of fluxes, Rods and fluxes for all purposes

Chapter 11 Welding	89

    Oxy-acetylene, Preheating, Cast Iron, Malleable Iron, Steel, Aluminum, Copper, Brass, Alloys, Gold and Silver

Chapter 12 Cutting	110

    Theory, Using the torch, The Vulcan torch, Instructions on Assembling

Chapter 13 Boiler and Sheet Metal Work	118

    Preheating, Repair Work, Corroded Mud Drums, Inserting new plates, Cutting door holes, man holes, etc, Patches, Welding in flues, Fabricating new work, Sanction of Boiler Insurance Companies

Chapter 14. Carbon Burning	126

    Theory, Cleaning Auto Cylinders

Useful Information and Tables	128

TABLES.

		Page
I	Elements, their symbols and atomic weights	12
II.	Weights of gases	21
III.	Average yield of gas from various grades of carbide	23
IV.	Heat conductivity of different metals	34
V.	Coefficients of expansion	33
VI.	Melting temperature of metals	39
VII.	Loss of pressure in pipes	70
VIII.	Loss of pressure by valves	71
IX.	Cost of oxyacetylene cutting	114
X	Cost of cutting with oxygen jet	128
XI.	Cost of welding with oxyacetylene torch	128
XII.	Quantity of gas in cylinders	129
XIII.	Variation of pressure in cylinders	129
XIV.	Comparison degrees Centigrade and Fahrenheit	130
XV.	Weight of oxygen drums	130
XVI.	Consumption of gas—and cost of oxyacetylene welding	131

LIST OF ILLUSTRATIONS.

Figure		Page
1	Broken locomotive cylinder	2
2	Same cylinder after welding	3
3	Building in gear teeth	5
4	Broken crank shaft	8
5	Same shaft after welding	9
6	Repairing broken pump case	10
7	Corner in chemical laboratory	15
8	Phases of combustion	17
9	Oxygen plant	18
10	Generator room in electrolytic oxygen plant	19
11	Electrolytic cells	20
12	High pressure pump for gas compression	29
14	Typical carbide to water generator	46
15	Modern oxyacetylene welding torch	50
16	Oxyacetylene torch	53
17	Straight line torch	53
18	Oxyacetylene cutting torch	54
19	Vulcan combination cutting and welding torch	55
20	Torch for welding machines	57
21	Automatic acetylene regulator	58
22	Automatic Oxygen Regulator	59

23	Oxyacetylene welding plant	60
30	Vulcan automatic acetylene generator	61
31	Vulcan generator welding plant	63
32	Interior of Vulcan generator	65
33	Vulcan portable generator plant	67
23	Welding table	75
24	Combination welding table	76
25	Oxygen valve on oxygen drum slowly	78
26	Removable base for oxygen drum	79
27	Portable plant using dissolved acetylene	82
28	Portable generator plant	84
29	Convenient time card	86
34-35	Practical method of beveling thin pieces	90
36	Method of beveling thick pieces	71
37-38	Illustrating economy of beveling on both sides	91
39-40	Effects of expansion and contraction	92
41	The melting rod should not	97
42	Circular movement of torch for work of medium thickness	98
43	Side to side movement of the torch for heavier welds	99
44	Position of torch for filling holes	100
45	Crank shaft on V blocks prepared for welding	107
46	Auto cylinder prepared for welding	108
47	Cutting machine	113
48	Cutting machine	114
49	Cutting floor beams	115
50	Cutting old boiler	116
51	Cutting old boiler	117
52		
53	Examples of Expansion	121
54		
55	Overcoming effects of expansion	121
56	Deformation caused by expansion	122
57		
58		
59		
60	Good and bad	
61	Examples of prepared joints	123
62		
63		
64		
65	Carbon burner at work	127
66	Fabricating a bosh jacket	120

VULCAN

VULCAN

The Roman God Of Fire

In olden days when Jupiter, the God of all other Gods, dwelt on the celebrated mountain Olympus, and presided over the ancient Romans, when Neptune dominated over the sea, and the beautiful Diana, with her maidens, cared for all the wild animals of the forest; there came to the family of Jupiter and his wife, Juno, a little son whom they called Vulcan.

Little Vulcan possessed great powers and ability, but he was not a handsome child and his mother Juno, who was disappointed in not having a more beautiful son to grace the home of the Gods, threw him down from Heaven. The infant God, falling into the sea, was rescued and adopted by Thetis, who kept him until he was nine years old, and then restored him to his parents.

Even in his youth, the little God displayed wonderful ability at the forge and all metallic handicrafts; and Jupiter, recognizing this wonderful ability, made him the God of Fire. He later erected forges and work shops in which he employed wonderful one-eyed giants, called the Cyclops, to assist him. In these shops he fabricated many great metal works, and one of his principal duties was to forge thunder bolts for his father Jupiter. Some claim his shops were on Mount Etna, where he used the heat of the volcano to work his forges.

Vulcan not only had the ability to make the hottest fires and forge the most difficult metal objects; but he was artistic by nature; so when Jupiter wished to provide the earth with the first mortal woman, Vulcan fashioned her out of clay, and the Gods animated the statue. So his wonderful work is handed down to the present day in the grace and beauty of our women.

In honor of this Roman God, we have dedicated this book and named our process, which develops the hottest flame known, and causes the hardest metals to flow like wax, to Vulcan the God of Fire and Patron of all metallic handicraft!

Vulcan Process Co.

WELDING AND CUTTING METALS
BY THE
OXYACETYLENE PROCESS

OXY-ACETYLENE WELDING AND CUTTING

FIG. 1.

BROKEN LOCOMOTIVE CYLINDER.

This illustration shows the cylinder after the edges of the fracture had been chipped for welding.

The bar across the front and a similar bar across the rear was used to support a temporary grate, upon which the preheating fire was built.

FIG. 2.

LOCOMOTIVE CYLINDER AFTER WELDING.

This illustrates the same cylinder shown in Fig. 1, with a new cast iron piece welded in the fracture. Ordinarily the old piece is used to make the mend, but in this case the old piece had been destroyed by repeated attempts to weld it in with thermit.

CHAPTER I.

THE USE OF THE OXY-ACETYLENE FLAME.

The oxy-acetylene welding and cutting torch has become so popular in the last few years, that almost every issue of the trade papers in any branch of work contains interesting accounts of new successes in the use of this powerful tool. The first application of the process, to commercial use, dates back to 1903, and its rapid growth in popularity is due to the ease and economy with which its intense heat is applied to any of the metal trades, to join two pieces by welding, or separate them by cutting without the stroke of a hammer.

A notable example of the saving that may be effected by using this process is in the event of repairing a broken locomotive cylinder shown in Fig. 1. This cylinder had a piece broken out of the wall including a portion of the flange. Previous attempts to weld this piece in place by other methods had proven disastrous, and resulted in making the fracture larger. The oxy-acetylene process was then brought into use, and in less than a day's time a new piece was welded in as shown in Fig. 2. The cylinder was rebored, drilled, and the job finished without removing it from the locomotive. A great saving in this case is credited to the fact that the locomotive was put back into service in a comparatively short time, and the repairs were made without dismantling. The durability of this work is illustrated in fact that this cylinder was welded July 10th, 1910, and is still in successful operation.

Very often small pieces of a machine are broken off and lost, and in consequence the whole machine is out of use. In such cases it is not always necessary to have the missing piece with which to make repairs, but the missing portion may be built on with similar material melted from the welding rod. A good example of cases where this process is appliable is in building new teeth into a broken gear or sprocket wheel, building up lugs or adding new material to parts that are badly worn. There are innumerable instances where the addition of a little metal will save much expense and long delays, and in the opera-

FIG. 3.

BUILDING IN GEAR TEETH.

In this process the old teeth are not required to make the mend, but new material is built up to form a new tooth.

tion of contractors who are remote from their base of supplies, this sometimes amounts to quite an item.

Large shipyards, railroad shops, contracting engineers, as well as the smaller institutions, machine shops, boiler shops, foundries, garages and blacksmiths, all find this powerful flame indispensable for sure, quick and economical results. In proof of this statement it is well to cite experiments made at different times, and in different places by two of our foremost railway systems. These experiments were very carefully conducted through a period of 14 days to ascertain to a certainty the exact economic value of this process. Every item of cost was carefully checked against the records of former methods, and the results showed an average saving of $155 a day, for each day the test continued.

This immense daily saving was made possible by having plenty of work on which to use the process, but the conditions were far from ideal, and it is safe to say, had the conditions been more favorable this figure could have been nearly doubled.

Another field where this tool is finding great favor is in cutting iron and steel structures, heavy plates, door holes or man holes in boilers, and in cutting up the wreckage of steel structures which have been destroyed by fire or wind. A recent incident where the oxy-acetylene torch proved to be valuable for this work, occurred in the harbor at Duluth where the wind destroyed several large steel docks It is difficult to imagine the bewildering entanglement of steel bars, beams and angles all piled up in a huge irregular mass. Heavy steel members were twisted and interlaced with smaller members in such a way that they could not be removed without cutting, and to cut them with a sharp edge tool was next to impossible The only tool suitable for this work was the oxy-acetylene cutting torch, and it was employed with very economic advantage.

Another occasion where this torch became conspicuous was in cutting up the wreckage of a steel freight steamer, which was sunk on the east coast about a year ago. The vessel had broken up and lay in pieces in about 30 feet of water. The pieces weighing 25 to 40 ton were a shapeless mass, with the plates, beams, and members bent and crumpled The plates forming the shell of the boat were about ⅝ in. thick at the top and on the sides, but on the bottom they were much heavier. The rivets could not be removed, since in many cases the flanges of angles and pieces of plates were bent over against them, preventing access to their heads. The condition of the steel was such that the expense of ordinary hand cutting would have been prohibitive, and the wreckage would have been a total loss had the oxy-acetylene torch not been available.

An idea may be formed of the speed and ease with which steel plates can be cut by this process from the following figures:

    Plates ½ inch thick—30 inches per minute.

    Plates 1 inch thick—20 inches per minute.

    Plates 1½ inch thick—16 inches per minute.

    Plates 2 inch thick—12 inches per minute.

This information is tabulated in the back of the book.

To obtain a comparison, in time and cost, between cutting by hand in the usual way, and doing the same work with the oxy-acetylene cutting torch, careful observations were made and recorded, as outlined. Cutting a full door patch for boiler by the old method required six hours time for a boiler maker and his helper at a cost of $4.04. Doing the same job with the cutting torch required nine minutes time of one man and cost 25c. Cutting a side sheet and door sheet by the old method, required eighteen hours for a boiler maker and his helper, and cost $12.15. Doing the same work with the cutting torch required one-half hours time of one man and cost 83c.

These two comparisons were not selected to favor one cause or the other, but were taken at random from a list of many similar operations.

FIG. 4.

BROKEN CRANK SHAFT.

The illustration shows a six inch crank shaft being brought into shop preparatory to welding.

The illustration Fig. 4 shows a crank shaft six inches in diameter and eleven feet long. It was **a member in a three** cylinder 100 H. P. producer gas engine, belonging to a single unit electric light plant, and was broken square off through one of the arms, totally disabling the entire plant. It was taken to a welding shop and with the oxy-acetylene torch the complete job was welded and ready to deliver in less than twenty-four hours, at a cost of about $26.00. A detail of this cost is as follows:

8 hours welding time ....@	35c —	$2.80
817 ft. Oxygen ....@	02c —	16.34
812 ft. Acetylene ....@	00.8c—	6.49
50 lbs. Charcoal ....@	01c —	.50

After cooling, the weld was found to be perfectly homogeneous in texture, void of fire-scale, or oxidation, and machined freely. This crank shaft has since been in heavy service for a year or more and is giving perfect satisfaction.

FIG. 5.

CRANK SHAFT AFTER WELDING.

The charcoal itemized in cost was used for preheating purposes. The little white cross indicates the place where the weld was made.

FIG. 6.

REPAIRING BROKEN PUMP CASE BY AUTOGENOUS WELDING.

In this illustration the plate which is shown bolted temporarily in the opening of the pump case, was used as a grating to support the preheating fire.

CHAPTER II.

CHEMISTRY

Origin. The practical part of this science existed previous to the theoretical; and may be traced to Tubal Cain, the father worker of metals, but by degrees, as men began to think they also began to observe and theorize.

Thinking men saw that a gross earthy matter, such as iron ore, became changed, by fire, into a hard metallic substance like iron, and upon these observations was built the most perfectly systematized and exact science of the day.

The Elements.—In the earth are millions of chemical compounds which are mixed together to form the air, the water, the minerals or animal and vegetable life, and all of these compounds are capable of being separated into more simple substances called "elements" For example water may be separated into hydrogen and oxygen. Acetylene gas may be separated into the simpler substances, carbon and hydrogen. In these examples the water and acetylene are chemical compounds, but the hydrogen, oxygen and carbon are elements and are not capable of being separated into more simple substances. These elements may be separated into atoms, but all the atoms of any one element are alike in size and weight, and are composed of the same single substance as the element which it composed. Then we may say that *an element is a single, simple substance, which is dissimilar to, and incapable of being separated into, any other substance.*

Chemical Symbols—The earlier chemists employed the signs of the planets to represent the metals; thus, silver was the moon, hence the expression "silvery moon," and the term "lunar caustic" for silver nitrate. In the modern science each of the elements are represented by one or two initial letters called "symbols" taken from the Latin name of the element. The symbol for iron is Fe, because the Latin name of iron is ferrum. That for oxygen is O; for hydrogen is H; for carbon is C; and for calcium is Ca.

A table of about one-half of the known elements is arranged below showing their symbols and atomic weights.

TABLE I.

ELEMENTS, THEIR SYMBOLS AND ATOMIC WEIGHTS.

Arsenic	As	75	Manganese	Mn	55
Barium	Ba	137.4	Molybdenum	Mo	96
Bismuth	Bi	208	Nickel	Ni	59
Boron	B	11	Nitrogen	N	14
Calcium	Ca	40	Oxygen	O	16
Carbon	C	12	Phosphorus	P	31
Chlorine	Cl	35 5	Potassium	K	39
Chromium	Cr	52	Silicon	Si	28.4
Cobalt	Co	59	Silver	Ag	108
Copper	Cu	63 6	Sodium	Na	23
Fluorine	F	19	Sulphur	S	32
Gold	Au	197	Tin	Sn	118.5
Hydrogen	H	1	Titanium	Ti	48
Iodine	I	127	Tungsten	Wo	184
Irone	Fe	56	Vanadium	V	51
Lead	Pb	207	Zinc	Zn	65.4
Magnesium	Mg	24			

Chemical Notation.—The principles upon which the modern chemical notation is founded, is that each symbol indicates one or more atoms of the element it represents, thus C, C2, C27 indicate respectively, one, two and twenty-seven atoms of carbon. Two symbols, placed side by side signifies that they are in close chemical union; thus CO signifies a compound containing an atom of carbon and an atom of oxygen. C2 H2 signifies that two atoms of carbon are in chemical union with two atoms of hydrogen, forming one molecule of acetylene. When symbols are separated by the sign + it signifies that the atoms thus separated are not in chemical union to form one substance; but are mingled and still exist as separate substances, thus C2 H2 + O2 signifies that one molecule of acetylene is mixed with two atoms of oxygen. A number placed on left of a group of symbols signifies that the whole group, as far as the next comma or plus +, is to be multiplied by it; thus 2 CO signifies that one atom of carbon and one atom of oxygen are combined to form one molecule of carbon monoxide and that two of those molecules are represented. The expression H2 + 2 CO, signifies that two atoms of hydrogen are

mingled with two molecules of carbon monoxide The sign =
signifies a reaction or the result of mingling the atoms or
molecules of different substances; thus, $C_2H_2 + O_2 = H_2 + 2CO$ signifies that if one molecule of acetylene becomes
mingled with two atoms of oxygen, there will be a chemical
union in which two atoms of carbon unite with two atoms
oxygen, forming two molecules of carbon monoxide and liberating the two atoms of hydrogen, which become mingled with
the monoxide in an uncombined state.

Chemical Affinity.—The attraction that causes elements to
unite and form new substances, like water, acetylene or carbon monoxide, and afterwards holds them together, is called
chemical affinity. Some elements apparently have no affinity
for each other, while others have a tremendous affinity. Some
elements have an affinity for each other under certain influences, and will unite forming new substances, but under
other influences this affinity may be destroyed and the substances separated again into their original elements. Some
of the more common influences which may effect the affinity
of elements are heat, pressure and an electric current.

To start chemical union it is sometimes only necessary to
mix two substances together and they will unite and form
a new substance. In this instance the elements are held together by affinity. If this substance be mingled with another
element under a different influence it may become separated
and one of its elements unite with the newly added element.
Take for instance acetylene, which is composed of two atoms
of hydrogen and two atoms of carbon held together by affinity Under ordinary conditions this union is stable and
the acetylene may be mixed with oxygen without forming
any new substance; but if heat or pressure is applied the carbon will leave the hydrogen and unite with the oxygen. The
result in case of applied pressure would be an explosion.

The Atomic Theory.—From the foregoing it is observed
that the union of atoms to form new substances is represented
by a group of symbols, to which are attached various signs

and figures. This group of symbols and figures is called a chemical formula. Let us study these formulas a little farther. Take for instance C2 H2, from the table of atomic weights we find the atomic weight of C = 12, and H = 1; then form this formula C2 H2 we may derive four thoughts:

(1) the formula represents 1 molecule of acetylene.

(2) one molecule of acetylene contains two atoms of carbon and two atoms of hydrogen.

(3) one molecule of acetylene is composed of 24 parts by weight of carbon, and 2 parts by weight of hydrogen

(4) by weight, acetylene contains 26 parts.

If the formula and atomic weights are known, the percentage of the composition may be calculated as follows:

C = 2 x 12 = 24 or 24 parts by weight of carbon
H = 2 x 1 = 2 or 2 parts by weight of hydrogen.

26 parts by weight in acetylene

$$\frac{24}{26} = .923 \text{ or } 92\% \text{ carbon by weight}$$

$$\frac{2}{26} = .07692 \text{ or } 8\% \text{ hydrogen by weight}$$

Valence.—Atoms differ with respect to the number of atoms of other elements with which they will combine. This difference in combining power is indicated by the term valence.

The valence of an element is the number of hydrogen atoms with which its atom will unite, or replace.

In water H2 O we find that one atom of oxygen will unite with two atoms of hydrogen, therefore we say the valence of oxygen is II. The valence of carbon is IV. and of calcium is II This means that one atom of carbon will unite with or replace four atoms of hydrogen, and an atom of calcium will unite with or replace two atoms of hydrogen.

The application of valence is useful in writing formulas and

CHEMISTRY

determining reactions. Thus, knowing that the valence of carbon is IV, we know each atom of carbon will unite with four atoms of hydrogen, and since the valence of oxygen is II each atom of oxygen will replace two atoms of hydrogen. Then in the reaction $C_2H_2 + O_2 = H_2 + 2\,CO$, as stated on page 14, we know the final H_2 will unite with one more atom of oxygen and the final $2\,CO$ will unite with two more atoms of oxygen.

The complete reaction may be expressed as follows:

$C_2H_2 + O_2 = H_2 + 2CO$
$H_2 + O = H_2O =$ one molecule water
$2\,CO + O_2 = 2\,(CO_2) =$ two molecules carbon dioxide

FIG. 7.
CORNER IN CHEMICAL LABORATORY.

Reaction.—The combination of elements to form a new substance is called reaction. The term expresses a chemical union in which the resulting substance has properties different from the elements which compose it.

If the elements are mingled without chemical union, there is said to be *no reaction* Thus if finely ground sulphur be mixed with finely ground iron no new properties are produced, and we say no reaction has taken place, but if we heat the mixture a chemical action takes place in which the elements unite to form a new substance Then we say there has been a reaction.

When reactions produce heat, they have chemical energy, which can be transferred into other forms of work. Not all reactions produce heat, but some are accompanied by a consumption of heat, and therefore use up energy, or rather they transform energy into chemical work. This heat energy is not lost for we can get it back by reversing the action.

Combustion.—Combustion is a reaction in which a fuel (combustible) unites with oxygen and produces heat. There are several elements that will react with oxygen in this way. Foremost among these are carbon, hydrogen and iron. When there is just the right amount of both oxygen and combustible to cause reaction, we have perfect combustion, but if there is an excess of either element, we have incomplete combustion Incomplete combustion always results in loss of heat.

Flame—When reaction is very rapid, the heat developed may cause the gaseous elements to glow like white hot iron. These glowing gases are flame. Flame has three distinct parts: the central or non-luminous part, where there is no combustion, but where the carbon begins to separate from the hydrogen; the second or luminous part, where the carbon is for a moment free and heated to a white heat; and the exterior part, which is the hottest, and where combusion is complete. The foregoing is true with the ordinary flame where the oxygen is derived from the atmosphere and combustion takes on the exterior; but in the oxy-acetylene flame the oxygen is supplied in a pure state and mingled with the combustible before it is ejected from the torch. This causes very rapid reaction and intense heat, and in this

CHEMISTRY

case, since the reaction is at the interior the hottest part is at the point of greatest illumination. It is easy now to understand of what importance is the form of the burner, and how we may modify it accordingly as we want light or heat. If we wish light the carbon must be protected for a moment while it is in the glowing state, but not long enough for it to pass off unconsumed. If, on the contrary, heat is desired, the carbon must be burned as rapidly as possible.

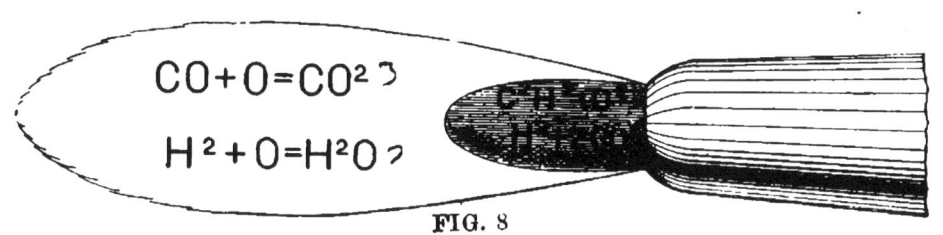

FIG. 8
PHASES OF COMBUSTION IN OXY-ACETYLENE FLAME.

Independent of the parts described on page 17, the oxy-acetylene flame is divided into two very distinguishable parts, the inner flame, where the oxygen, supplied by the torch, reacts with the carbon in the acetylene, producing carbon monoxide, and setting the hydrogen free, and the outer flame where the carbon monoxide and hydrogen reacts with the oxygen supplied by the atmosphere. The inner flame is of a dazzling white, but the outer flame has a bluish tinge, due to the combustion of hydrogen, surrounded by a yellow flame due to the combustion of carbon monoxide. The temperature, taken at the extremity of the white jet, is very much higher than that of any other flame, and is calculated to be 6300 degrees F.

To attain this temperature without waste of gases, the torch must be constructed on highly scientific principles. The size of the openings, the mixing chamber, pressures of gases, are all factors to be considered in its design.

OXYGEN.

Oxygen is an odorless, colorless, tasteless gas. It is mingled with nitrogen in the air, and combined with hydrogen in water. It is united with nearly all the minerals in their native state, and is the most abundant element known to us. At ordinary temperatures it forms few chemical reactions, but when heated, is one of the most active elements, vigorously reacting with hydrogen and carbon, as well as their compounds in the form of gases.

When oxygen reacts with an element the product is called an oxide, and the process is said to be oxidation. When iron is red hot it oxidizes very rapidly. The welder should therefore adjust his torch to procure a perfectly neutral flame, with just enough oxygen to consume the acetylene.

Oxygen is prepared in a variety of ways, giving as great a variety in percentage of purity. For commercial purposes it may be made from chlorate of potash and manganese dioxide in the proportions of 100 pounds of the chlorate of potash to 13 pounds of the manganese dioxide. These two chemicals are first thoroughly mixed, and then placed in a retort and heated. This liberates the oxygen, which passes off through washers to storage tanks. The cost of producing oxygen in this way, depends on the price of chemicals. With chlorate of potash at 9½c per pound and manganese dioxide at 2¾c per pound, the cost would average 4c per cubic foot, including cartage, shop expense, etc.

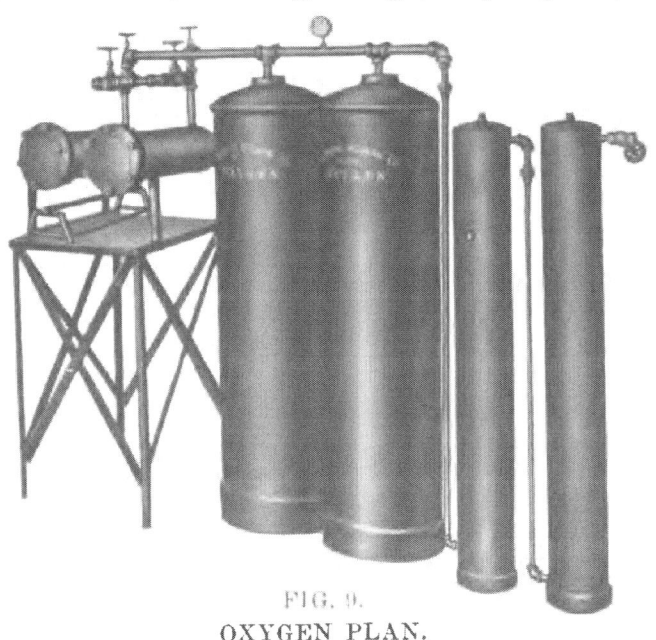

FIG. 9.
OXYGEN PLAN.
Using Crystallized Chlorate of Potash and Manganese Dioxide.

Oxygen from Air.—Oxygen may also be extracted from air. If, by means of combined pressure and cold, air be converted into a liquid, its two components may be separated by centrifugal force, or else the nitrogen may be allowed to evaporate leaving the liquid oxygen behind. No chemical processes are necessary for this separation because the elements are not combined.

FIG. 10.
GENERATOR ROOM IN ELECTROLYTIC OXYGEN PLANT.

Oxygen by Electrolysis of Water.—Oxygen and hydrogen are liberated when an electric current is passed through acidulated water. The apparatus first used for this purpose consisted of a vessel containing water and having suspended therein, two test tubes with their open end submerged. Positive and negative electrodes were placed just beneath the opening in the tubes, and when an electric current was caused to flow through the water between the electrodes, oxygen was liberated at the negative pole, and hydrogen at the positive pole. These gases ascended and were gathered in the tubes.

Although the production of oxygen and hydrogen, by the electrolysis of water, is one of the oldest electrochemical experiments, it was not until recent years that the process was made economically practical. There was considerable difficulty in developing an apparatus that would operate successfully in practice. One of the hardest conditions to meet was the necessity of absolute safety. The problem has now been worked out satisfactorily so that large scale electrolysis of water is on a solid industrial basis. Oxygen made by this process is most pure and best adapted to oxy-acetylene welding.

FIG. 11.
ELECTROLYTIC CELLS FOR GENERATING OXYGEN.

Hydrogen.

Hydrogen is a colorless, tasteless, odorless gas, and the lightest substance known. By weight it forms 11 per cent of water, and 8 per cent of acetylene. Hydrogen also exists in all living forms. It has a high chemical affinity for oxygen, and burns

CHEMISTRY

with it at a temperature of about 4100 degrees F. When used in the cutting torch with oxygen it is a very satisfactory fuel for cutting the ferrous metals. Hydrogen is obtained in its purest form by the electrolysis of water.

NITROGEN.

Nitrogen is a colorless, tasteless, odorless gas, forming 77 per cent of air. It is of no benefit to the oxy-acetylene welder, in fact it is a detriment since it does not support combustion but absorbs heat from the flame.

TABLE II
WEIGHTS OF GASES.

Name of Gas	At 32° F and 14.7 lbs pressure		
	Specific Gravity	Volume of one pound cubic foot	Weight of one cubic foot
Oxygen	1.104	11.2056	.08925
Air	1.	12.388	.08073
Hydrogen	.069	178.891	.00559
Nitrogen	.972	12.7226	.0786
Acetylene	.91	13.6126	.07346

CALCIUM CARBIDE

Calcium is the metal that exists in lime. Its symbol is Ca. Carbon, a solid but not a metal, occurs in the earth in crystallized form as graphite and as diamonds. It is also the fuel element in coal. The symbol for Carbon is C.

Calcium Carbide (CaC_2) is a compound of Calcium and Carbon in the proportions of 62 per cent calcium to 38 per cent carbon which combine to form a hard crystalline substance of a dark gray color. *In describing the manufacture of calcium carbide it is well for the reader to remember that the materials employed are among the most refactory ones which we know Lime is so infusible that it is frequently employed for the material of crucibles in which the highest melting metals are fused, and

*From bulletin of the department of chemistry. Pennsylvania State College.

for pencils in the calcium light, because it is capable of withstanding extremely high temperatures. Carbon is the material employed in the manufacture of arc lights, and other electric appliances for the same reason. Yet in the manufacture of carbide these two most refractory substances are forced into combination with each other.

It is the excessively high temperature attainable in the modern electric furnace, five to seven thousand degrees Fahrenheit, which alone accomplishes the combination of these elements to form calcium carbide.

The electric arc being formed in the furnace, a thoroughly incorporated mixture of coke and lime in the right proportion is introduced. The change which takes place is

$$CaO + 3C = CaC_2 + CO$$

which means that fifty-six pounds of lime, and thirty-six of coke make 64 pounds of carbide, and liberate twenty-eight of carbon monoxide, a gas which escapes or is burned at the mouth of the furnace. Thus, for each pound of carbide made, there is consumed a pound and a half of a mixture which is something like seven-twelfths lime with five-twelfths coke.

Granted pure material, there is formed an ingot of very pure carbide, surrounded by a crust of less pure product because partially unconverted.

In breaking up, packing and shipping the carbide, this poorer crust is rejected. At first impure materials were employed for the manufacture of carbide, but this resulted in an inferior grade, which in turn yielded an impure gas, so that at the present time it is everywhere recognized as essential, that only first class materials should be used.

It is customary to use lime that is 99 per cent pure, and coke of low ash. Both must contain as little sulphur and phosphorus as possible.

Carbide decomposes with water in accordance with the following chemical equation:

$$CaC_2 + 2H_2O = C_2H_2 + Ca(OH)_2$$

A pound of absolutely pure carbide will yield 5½ feet of

acetylene, but absolute purity is not a practical commercial possibility In practice good carbide may be expected to produce never less than four cubic ft. and rarely more than five cubic ft. of acetylene gas per pound of carbide. The table on page 23 gives the gas yield of various grades carbide.

TABLE III.
THE AVERAGE YIELD OF GAS.
From the Various Grades of Carbide.

Grade 3½x2	4½ cubic feet
Grade 2 x ½	4½ cubic feet
Grade 1¼x ⅜	4½ cubic feet
Grade ¼x1/12	4 cubic feet
Grade Electrolite	4 cubic feet

Calcium Carbide is a safe substance to store or transport under proper conditions. It cannot explode, take fire, or otherwise do harm, unless exposed to moisture. In that event the water in the moisture will slowly liberate acetylene which in the presence of flame, will ignite.

ACETYLENE.

Acetylene is a colorless, tasteless gas, possessed of a peculiar penetrating odor. It is a compound of two atoms of carbon to two atoms of hydrogen, and is known by the formula C_2H_2. Being composed of these two elements only, it belongs to a class of compounds known as hydro-carbons. All hydro-carbons are combustible and acetylene will explode when only 3⅓ per cent is mixed with air. Its ignition point is lower than coal gas, being about 900 degrees F against 1100 degrees required to ignite coal gas. It burns in air with a brilliant but smoky flame, uniting with the oxygen of the air, in the following proportions.

$$2 C_2H_2 + 5O_2 = 4 CO_2 + 2 H_2O$$

Acetylene is an endothermic compound. In its formation heat is absorbed, and there resides in the acetylene molecules the power of spontaneously decomposing and liberating this heat if subjected to temperatures or pressure beyond the capacity of its unstaple nature to withstand. Acetylene is decomposed into its constituent elements at a critical temperature of approximately 1400 degrees F., or at the critical pressure of two atmospheres (29.4 pounds) at which pressure it becomes dangerous.

Acetylene, without the mixture of air or oxygen, at ordinary pressures, is not explosive in any sense, except as referred to above.

When acetylene is used in the blow torch it combines with oxygen in equal volumes and liberates much heat. The temperature of the oxy-acetylene flame, taken at the extremity of the white jet, is very much higher than that of any other flame. It is calculated to be 6300 degrees F. In all cases the white jet of the oxy-acetylene flame can melt lime, the melting point of which is estimated at 5432 degrees.

CHAPTER III.

PHYSICS

Pneumatics.—Pneumatics is that branch of mechanics which treats of the properties of gases and air

It was supposed by the ancients that air was inponderable. that it weighed nothing, and it was not until the year 1650 that it was proven that air really had weight A cubic foot of air under ordinary conditions, weighs about eight one-hundredths of a pound. Since air has weight it is evident that the enormous quantity of air that constitutes the atmosphere must exert considerable pressure on the earth. By experiment and calculation this pressure has been determined to be 14.7 pounds per square inch.

In the strictest sense of the word, air is not a gas, but is a mixture of gases and consists of about 23 parts oxygen and 77 parts nitrogen, by weight; or 21 parts oxygen and 79 parts nitrogen, by volume. Its physical characteristics are the same as the gases, and in this respect it is classified among them.

The most striking feature concerning gases is that, no matter how small the quantity may be they will always fill the vessels which contain them, and if the temperature of the confined gas remains the same, the pressure and volume will always vary the same way. The law which expresses this is called Boyle's Law, and is as follows:

Boyle's Law.—*The temperature remaining constant the volume of a given quantity of gas varies inversely as the pressure.*

The meaning of this is: If the size of the containing vessel is diminished to ½ or ⅓ of its former volume, the pressure of the gas will be increased to 2 or 3 times its original pressure. It also means that if the size of the containing vessel is increased to 2 or 3 times its original volume, the pressure will diminish to ½ or ⅓ of the former pressure.

In these and the following statements the reader should not confuse the words volume and quantity. The volume will correspond with the cubic capacity of the vessel, while the quantity will represent the amount of air or gas contained in the vessel under pressure.

Suppose a steel drum is such a size that it will measure exactly 3 cubic feet. If it is open to the air it is evident the drum will contain 3 cubic feet of air at atmospheric pressure. Then if twice as much air, or 6 feet is put into the drum, the pressure will be doubled to 29.4 pounds, and if one hundred times as much air or 300 feet is put into the drum the pressure will be raised 100 times and become 1470 pounds. Now if half of this air, or 150 feet, is drawn out, the pressure will be reduced to one-half of 1470 pounds and become 735 pounds.

As a necessary consequence of Boyle's law, it may be stated that, *the quantity of gas in a given size drum, varies directly as the pressure.*

Knowing the quantity of gas a drum will contain under certain pressure, the quantity for any other pressure may be calculated by the following simple formula in which

A = the nominal rated pressure
B = pressure of gas in drum
C = capacity of drum under A pressure
X = contents of drum in cubic feet of gas

$$\text{Then } \frac{CB}{A} = X$$

Expressing this formula in words, we have the rule.

Multiply the rated capacity of the drum by the pressure of gas in the drum and divide by the nominal rated pressure to find the contents of the drum.

Suppose an oxygen drum contains 200 feet of gas at 1800 pounds pressure, and after being used for sometime the pressure has diminished to 700 pounds. If we wished to learn the quantity of gas still remaining in the drum, the calculation would be as below.

$$\frac{200 \times 700}{1800} = 77 \frac{77}{100} \text{ feet}$$

In all that has been said before, it has been stated that the temperature was constant, the reason for this will now be explained. Suppose a definite quantity of air at 32 degrees F. be placed in a cylinder with a movable piston and that this piston is weighted to cause the air to be at a constant uniform pressure. If the temperature of the air within the cylinder be raised to 33 degrees F. it will be found that the piston has raised a certain amount, consequently the volume has increased while the pressure remained the same. If more heat is applied and the temperature raised to 34 degrees F. it will be found the piston has raised again, and that every increase in temperature will cause a corresponding increase in volume. The law that expresses this change is called Gay-Lusac's Law, and is expressed as follows:

Gay Lusac's Law.—*If the pressure remains constant every increase of temperature of 1 degree F. produces, in a given quantity of gas, an expansion of $\frac{1}{492}$ of its volume at 32 degrees F.*

If the pressure remains constant it will be found that every decrease of 1 degree F. will cause a decrease of $\frac{1}{492}$ of the volume at 32 degrees F.

According to the modern and now generally accepted theory of heat, the atoms and molecules of all bodies are in an incessant state of vibration. The vibratory movement in gases is faster than in liquids, and in liquids it is faster than in solids. Any increase in heat increases the vibrations, and a decrease in heat decreases them. From calculation and experiment, it has been concluded that all vibration ceases at a temperature of 460 degrees below zero. This point is called *absolute zero*, and all temperatures reckoned from this point are called *absolute temperatures.*

When the word temperature alone is used the meaning is the same as ordinarily applied, but when absolute temperature is specified, 460 degrees F. must be added to the temperature. The absolute temperature corresponding to 32 degrees F. is 460 + 32 = 492 dgrees F.

In calculating the effect of an increasing or decreasing temperature, upon the volume or pressure of gases, the temperature is reckoned from absolute zero.

Suppose a steel drum is charged with 200 cubic feet of gas at 1800 pounds pressure, and at a temperature of 68 degrees F.; and subsequently the temperature is raised to 100 degrees F. The increase in pressure may be calculated by the following formula in which

A = the nominal rated pressure of the drum at 68 degrees Fahrenheit.

T = the absolute temperature of 68 degrees F.

t = absolute temperature of gas in drums

E = pressure of gas at t temperature

$$\text{Then } \frac{t}{T} A = E$$

FIG. 12.

HIGH PRESSURE PUMP FOR GAS COMPRESSION.

Three cylinder hydraulic pump having capacity to compress 12 cubic feet of gas per minute from 1,500 pounds to 2,200 pounds pressure per square inch.

Expressing this formula in words we have the rule. *Divide the absolute temperature of the gas in the drums by the absolute temperature of 68 degrees F., and multiply the quotient by the nominal rated pressure of the drum, to find the pressure due to a change in temperature.*

This final pressure is computed as shown.

$$460 + 100 = 560$$
$$460 + 68 = 528$$
$$\frac{560}{528} = 1.06$$

$$1.06 \times 1800 = 1908 = \text{final pressure}$$

Heat.—As to the exact nature of heat, scientists differ, but all modern thinkers and investigators agree that *heat is a form of energy.* It is not proposed here to enter into the different theories regarding heat, but this much of the generally accepted theory is given to make clear the principles which are to follow.

To avoid possible misunderstanding the attention of the reader is first directed to the difference between the quantity and intensity of heat. This difference is easier explained by a series of illustrative statements.

The same amount or *quantity* of heat may be delivered to equal amounts of different materials without having the same sensible effect.

Equal weights of different substances, having the same temperature may be placed in an oven and be subjected to the same heat for the same length of time, and their final *temperature* will be considerably different, although each has received the same *quantity* of heat.

Then it is clear that the same *quantity* of heat will not raise the same weight of different materials to the same *temperature.*

Reversing this experiment we find that if equal weights of different substances be heated to the same *temperature* and plunged into vessels containing like quantities of water at like temperatures, the water in the different vessels will not be raised to the same degree of temperature.

Then it is clear that these various substances actually contained different *quantities* of heat at the same *temperature.*

Unit of Heat. The standard with which quantities of heat are measured is called the *heat unit,* and represents the amount of heat required to raise a certain amount of water one degree in temperature. Different communities use the same general methods for determining heat units, but vary the amount of water to suit the convenience of their national standards, therefore it was found necessary to distinguish between the methods in which different standards are employed.

The British Thermal Unit —The quantity of heat required to raise one pound of water one degree Fahrenheit, is called a British Thermal Unit. Instead of writing out the words British Thermal unit in full it is customary to abbreviate them B. T. U.

The Calorie.—The quantity of heat required to raise one kilogram of water one degree Centigrade is called a Calorie.

One calorie is equal to 3.96 B. T. U.

Temperature.—The word temperature expresses the sensible heat which a substance possesses, and is measured by comparison with some other substance having the same amount of sensible heat. For convenience and for scientific purposes, two scales of comparison are employed. Both scales are compared with the same substance at the same temperatures, the only difference being in the graduations of the scales. These are called the Fahrenheit and Centigrade scales.

Thermometers.—The instrument on which these comparative scales are arranged to measure temperature is called a thermometer. The divisions of the scale are called *degrees,* the substance with which they are compared is water, and the temperature at which they are compared is the freezing point and boiling point.

Fahrenheit—On the Fahrenheit scale the freezing point of water is marked 32. and the boiling point 212. and the intervening space divided into 180 equal parts called degrees. Thirty-two degrees are marked off on the lower end of the scale, and called zero. So in speaking of water we would say that it freezes at 32 degrees above zero, and boils at 212 degrees above zero.

As many degrees are marked above the boiling point or below zero, as are desired.

Centigrade.—In graduating a Centigrade scale, the freezing point is marked zero, the boiling point 100, and the intervening space is divided into 100 equal degrees.

It will be observed that 100 degrees Centigrade covers the same range of temperature as 180 degrees Fahrenheit, therefore, one degree centigrade equals one and eight-tenths degrees Fahheit.

Temperatures designated by one scale may be converted to the other scale by formulas.

When F = degrees Fahrenheit
and C = degrees Centigrade
Then $1.8 C + 32 = F.$
$$\frac{F - 32}{1.8} = C.$$

Expansion.—The volume of any substance is always changed when the temperature is changed; nearly all of them expand when heated, and contract when cooled. This phenomenom causes the welder considerable trouble unless it is thoroughly understood, and it is well for him to give this subject much thought and study, for his success depends to a great extent, on his ability to overcome the effects of expansion and contraction. The method of overcoming these effects will be treated fully under the subject of welding

Suppose that a bar of iron is exactly 10 feet long at a **temperature of 50 degrees F.**, if the temperature be raised to 60 degrees it will be found that it has lengthened a definite amount. If the temperature is then raised to 70 degrees it will be found to have lengthened exactly the same amount as before. This is true of all metals Each metal will expand a certain definite amount with every degree increase in temperature, and when cooling they contract at precisely the same ratio; but the different metals do not expand with the same ratio as compared one with the other.

The ratio of expansion of the different metals has been determined and the amount of expansion of one inch in length for one degree temperature has been tabulated into a table called *coefficients of expansion*. These seem like small amounts, but when the temperatures are high the amount of expansion is an item to be considered.

TABLE V.

COEFFICIENTS OF EXPANSION FOR VARIOUS SUBSTANCES.

Cast Iron	.00000617
Copper	.00000955
Brass	.00001037
Silver	.00000690
Bar Iron	.00000686
Steel (untempered)	.00000599
Steel (tempered)	.00000702
Aluminum	.0000129
Zinc	.00001634
Tin	.00001410
Mercury	.00003334
Alcohol	.00019259

If a bar of cast iron 48 in. long is heated from 50 degrees F. to a bright red, or 1250 degrees F, the amount it will expand may be determined by formula in which,

A = length of bar in inches

B = the raise in temperature

C = coefficient of expansion

D = amount of expansion in inches

Then A. B. C. = D.

Expressing this formula in words we have the rule.

Multiply the length of the bar in inches by the number of degrees raise in temperature, and multiply the product by the coefficient of expansion, to find the amount of expansion in inches. The coefficient of expansion for cast iron is .00000617 Using this figure and multiplying as directed we find,

48 x 1200 x .00000617 = .355392 or 3/8 of an inch.

If the bar mentioned has a section of 3 square inches, and forms one of the arms in a gear, with one end attached to the hub and the other end in the rim, it will, when heated, exert a thrust of

135 tons against the rim. It is useless to try to resist this enormous pressure, and the only way to avoid trouble is to heat other portions of the gear so that all parts will expand together. In the parlance of the welder, this method is called *preheating*.

Expansion extends in all directions. If a steel plate four feet square is heated red hot it will become ⅜ of an inch wider, and ⅜ of an inch longer; and when it cools it will contract the same amount. If the edges are welded solid while the plate is hot, the strain caused by contraction will amount to many tons

The amount of the expansion depends on the temperature, and extent of the heated portion. If a bar of metal is heated in the center, the heat will be greatest at the point where the heat is applied. Some of this heat will be conducted through the bar, and some will radiate to the air. The distance to which it will be conducted through the bar depends on the speed at which the bar will conduct it as compared with the rate of radiation.

If bars of different metals are heated in the center the distance to which the heat will travel in the various bars will be greatest in the metals that are the best conductors, and since the extent of the heated portion is one of the determining factors of expansion it follows, *When bars of different metals have heat applied to a limited section, the best conductors will be expanded most, if other factors are equal.*

Silver stands foremost among the metals as a conductor of heat. Representing the conductivity of silver by 100 the following table shows the conducting power of some of the metals.

TABLE IV
HEAT CONDUCTIVITY OF DIFFERENT METALS

Metal	Value	Metal	Value
Silver	100.00	Iron	11.9
Copper	73.6	Steel	11.6
Gold	53.2	Lead	8.5
Aluminum	31.3	Platinum	8.4
Brass	23.1	Rose's Alloy	2.8
Zinc	19.0	Bismuth	1.8
Tin	14.5		

CHAPTER IV.
METALS AND THEIR PROPERTIES.

The Ferrous Group.—Pure iron is a white metal and one of the chemical elements, and although it is with one exception the commonest and most abundant metal in the earth it never occurs in nature in the pure metallic form, but is always united with oxygen, neither does it exist as an article of commerce, but appears on the market contaminated with carbon, silicon, and other impurities forming cast iron, wrought iron, or steel. These three products comprise the ferrous group, and are the largest manufactured product in the world.

Iron has a chemical affinity for oxygen and carbon. The former element is ruinous and destructive, but the latter element gives it greater strength and at the same time makes it harder and more brittle. So important is the influence of carbon in controlling the characteristics of the ferrous metals, that they are classified according to the amount of carbon in them. When melted in the presence of these elements it combines with them very rapidly, and their effect on the metal should be constantly borne in mind when we are using an oxy-acetylene torch, for an excess of either oxygen or acetylene gas will contribute oxygen or carbon to the melted metal.

Cast Iron.—Cast iron is the most impure of the ferrous products, and in consequence it is comparatively weaker, more brittle and melts at a lower temperature than wrought iron or steel. A typical example of cast iron would contain about 93½ per cent pure iron, 3½ per cent carbon and 3 per cent other impurities. Its tensile strength would be about 23000 pounds, and its melting point about 2200 degrees Fahrenheit. In solidifying from the molten condition to the temperature of the air it shrinks or shortens about one-eighth of an inch to every foot in length, or when in the solid state it shrinks about one sixty-fourth of an inch for every 200 degrees decrease in temperature. This feature requires the serious consideration of the welder, for when cast iron is solidifying it is in its very weakest state, and unless this shrinkage or contraction is provided for, cracks will ensue.

Another feature which may cause trouble to the welder, is the transfer of carbon from the graphite to the combined form by rapid cooling from the molten condition

Carbon is contained in solidified cast iron in two forms, the graphitic form in which free carbon is mechanically mixed with the iron in little flakes of graphite; and the combined form, in which the carbon is chemically united with the iron. In the graphitic form it does not effect the hardness of iron, but in the combined form it will cause the iron to be hard or soft according to the amount contained in it.

The welder should remember that carbon is always in the combined state with iron when the mass is in a molten condition, and as it cools graphite precipitates, but this cooling must be very slow for the change to take place since it is a very sluggish change and requires several seconds for its accomplishment; but on the contrary if the mass is cooled rapidly this precipitation of graphite is prevented and a metal is obtained in which all the carbon is in the combined form, producing an iron that may be as brittle as glass and so hard that it cannot be machined or filed This rapid cooling, which is called chilling, may be accomplished by dropping the melted iron on to a cold metal surface, and the resultant hard cast iron is called chilled iron.

Malleable Cast Iron is first cast in the condition of very hard, brittle white cast iron. It has less carbon and silicon in its composition than other cast iron, and when poured in the moulds which give it the desired shape it is rapidly cooled so that nearly all the carbon it contains is in the combined form. It can be readily understood from the preceding paragraph that if this combined carbon can be precipitated to graphite the casting will be softer, and furthermore if the size of these flakes of graphite can be reduced the casting will be stronger because the smaller are the planes of easy rupture. Being softer and stronger it may be bent and is called malleable.

Eliminating and changing the carbon in white cast iron to make it malleable is accomplished by prolonged heat treatment and the process, which is called annealing, is performed after the iron has been cast into moulds and cooled. They are then cleaned and packed in iron boxes with some pulverized substance containing oxide of iron, such as iron ore, or mill scale, placed in an annealing furnace and heated to a temperature of 1300 degrees, and at this temperature they are kept for many hours While under this heat there occurs the precipitation of graphite. which normally would have occurred during solidification, and in the majority of cases nearly all of the combined carbon is changed to graphite, or eliminated by uniting with the oxygen in the material used for packing.

Under this treatment the graphite does not form in flakes as in ordinary cast iron, but forms in minute particles which are not nearly so weakening or embrittling to the casting as flakes of graphite would be. The whole annealing process requires about six days of continuous firing, and should not be attempted by persons who are not familiar with the chemistry of iron, or who do not possess an equipment of furnace, iron packing boxes and packing.

Since malleable iron is always cast in the form of hard white iron and subsequently made malleable by a process applied to its exterior, it follows that the change of structure is more complete at the surface giving the outside the texture of mild steel, while the middle portion may resemble a very soft cast iron. It is this peculiarity which frustrates the efforts of the amateur welder.

Wrought Iron —Wrought iron is almost the same as very low carbon steel, its chief distinction being in the method of refining rather than the composition of the metal. It is made by melting pig iron, steel scrap and other ferrous materials in contact with iron ore, and burning out the impurities, leaving metallic iron. This iron is not in a melted state when finished, for the temperature of the furnace is not sufficiently high to keep it fluid after the carbon has been burned. It is in a pasty condition and when taken out of the furnace is a honey-comb of iron with each cell filled with melted lava This honey-comb is then squeezed and rolled until most of the slag is worked out and the iron frame work welded together in a crude rough bar. These bars, which are an intermediate product, called "muck bars", are then cut into lengths, "piled", heated to a welding heat and rolled again, and after this second rolling they become the "merchant iron" of commerce.

The finished bar contains less than .12 per cent carbon and about 1.5 per cent slag. Some think that this slag serves as a flux and assists in welding, but this is doubtful. It is more probable that the easy welding of wrought iron is due alone to its being low in carbon.

Steel.—In olden times all kinds of steel, whether made in the crucible, in the cementation chamber or in the puddle furnace, contained carbon enough to make them suitable for cutting tools when hardened in water, and the steels that were later made in the Bessemer converter during the early days of its history were all more or less hard, much of it being used for tools; consequently the metal made in the converter was called Bessemer steel.

As time went on and the cost of operation was reduced below that of making wrought iron, a great deal of very soft metal was made in the converter and open-hearth furnace. It was impossible to draw the line between this steel and the earliest products of the converter, so practical men in America and Europe did not try to do so, but called everything that was made in the converter, or in the open-hearth, or in the crucible by the name of steel, although the product may at times resemble wrought iron, and it is a fact that the method by which steel is made cannot be discovered by ordinary chemical analysis.

The primitive Tubal Cain could produce a hard cutting instrument with no apparatus save a wrought iron bar and a pile of charcoal; and the natural developments have led to the conclusion that a given content of carbon will confer a greater hardness and strength, with less accompanying brittleness than any other element.

There is such a widely varying quantity of carbon and other alloys in steel, accompanied by as wide a range of physical properties, that the subject cannot be treated in a book of this kind; but before leaving the subject it is well to speak of a process by which hard tool steel may be made, which has not heretofore been mentioned. This is known as the "cementation" or "blister" process and is undoubtedly the one used by Tubal Cain as mentioned in the preceding paragraph. Blister steel is made by placing bars of very pure iron in long pots with charcoal and exposing them to about 1300 degrees heat. This heat is maintained for about ten days and when the bars are removed they are graded according to their carbon content which ranges from .5 to 1.5 per cent. Although this process is expensive, it produces a very fine grade steel and it is still being used in Sheffield, England.

This process is mentioned here to remind the welder, that unless he uses a perfectly neutral flame, it is possible to carbonize his weld, and form a scale that cannot be machined. In other words, if he uses more acetylene gas than his oxygen can consume, the carbon of the unburned acetylene may unite with the iron by a process somewhat similar to the blister process.

Like other metals steel expands and contracts with heat or cold, and the amount of this expansion is about one sixty-fourth of an inch for every 250 degrees change of temperature.

TABLE VI.

MELTING TEMERATURE OF METALS.

Name of Metal	Temperature C	Temperature F	Name of Metal	Temperature C	Temperature F
Tin	223	449	White Cast Iron	1100	2012
Lead	327	621	Gray Cast Iron	1200	2192
Zinc	419	786	Hard Steel	1400	2552
Aluminum	657	1212	Mild Steel	1471	2680
Bronze	900	1652	Nickel	1484	2703
Brass	950	1742	Wrought Iron	1500	2730
Silver	961	1762	Platinum	1776	3232
Copper	1065	1949	Iridium	2000	3632
Gold	1065	1949			

Copper.

Copper is the only metal which occurs free in large, widely distributed deposits. For this reason, it was the first metal exclusively used by man. The copper age followed the stone age. The island of Cyprus was noted in the time of the Romans for its production of copper, or as it was then called, Cyprian brass

We obtain the symbol Cu. from the Latin name, Cuprum.

The noted mines of native copper in Michigan, along the south shore of Lake Superior, were extensively worked before Columbus discovered America.

From them masses of copper of enormous size, one of which weighed nearly five hundred tons, have been obtained. These mines are still an important source of copper.

Copper has a characteristic reddish color Only two of the common metals, gold and silver, surpass it in malleability and ductility, and it stands next to silver in as a conductor of electricity and heat.

The tensile strength, which is about 33,000 lbs. per square inch at ordinary temperatures, decreases rapidly under the effect of heat At 932 degrees it is only about 14000 lbs. per square inch. When copper is melted it oxidizes rapidly in contact with air, and this oxide is very soluble in the metal; it forms with it an alloy, which crystallizes with the mass on cooling. Melted copper also absorbs hydrogen and carbon monoxide which are present in the oxy-acetylene flame, and on cooling, the metal is riddled with blow holes. The effect of this oxidation and absorbtion of gases, can only be overcome by the use of fluxes and alloys in the welding rod.

Brass.

Brasses are alloys of copper and zinc. They do not conduct heat so readily as copper, but their tensile strength when hot is much higher than copper. The reader will note the great difference in melting points in the two principal elements in brass. Zinc melts at 786 degrees F. and vaporizes at 1684 degrees, while the melting point of copper is 1949 degrees, or 265 degrees higher than the vaporization temperature of zinc. When brass is melted under the direct action of the flame, this vaporization of zinc is very pronounced. The copper in brass also retains its property of absorbtion and oxidation So we say that the melting of brass under the action of the torch is attended by three distinct phenomena · Absorbtion of gases; volatilization of zinc; and oxidation.

These difficulties are overcome by use of the proper welding rods.

Alloys.

*According to the authoritive definition. "a metalic alloy is a substance possessing the general physical properties of a metal, but consisting of two or more metals, or of metals with non-metallic bodies, in intimate mixture, solution, or combination, forming when melted, a homogeneous fluid.

In plain language, this means that, when melted, the different components are dissolved in one another. Metal alloys therefore, come under the general heading of solutions. In fact the great bulk of our alloys, are produced by first dissolving the melted components and then allowing them to freeze. The law governing this freezing, or solidification, have only been known a few years, and this new knowledge has made great revolution in physical chemistry.

In perfect alloys, the solid solution bears the same relation to the melted solution as a pure solid metal does to the same metal when melted. Consequently any solution of these metals will cool to the freezing point, without there being any important change in their relation.

The reason that these solid solutions form in any proportion is that the two metals crystallize alike. It is, perhaps, a new thought to the reader, but it is true, that a metal forms a crystal when it solidifies. Furthermore, each metal has a particular, general shape which its crystals assume, and there is no force powerful enough to prevent them from taking this shape in preference to any other.

Tiny as the crystals sometimes are, often requiring the highest powers of the microscope to reveal them, their crystalline forces are very powerful. If, therefore, two metals do not form like crystals, they cannot solidify in solution, i. e., in the same crystal,

*From Metallurgy of Iron and Steel, by Bradley Stoughton.

but crystallization (i. e, freezing) must be accomplished by precipitation, or separation into two distinct substances."

There are a great number of alloys all having different physical properties, and this difference is sometimes due to the presence of an element in very small proportions. When melted the components of an alloy sometimes react with the flame in entirely different ways, and unless welding rods and fluxes are used, which will compensate for this reaction, the entire structure of the alloy may become changed. The welder should therefore carefully adhere to the instructions given on welding the various alloys.

On the following page is given a list of alloys, their composition and proportions.

Sb. = Antimony, Bi = Bismuth, Cu = Copper, Au. = Gold, Fe. = Iron, Pb. = Lead, Ni. = Nickle, Ag. = Silver, Su. = Tin, Zn = Zinc.

TABLE OF ALLOYS.

Name of Alloy.	Proportion by weight.
Brass, common yellow	2 Cu, 1 Zn
Brass, to be rolled	32 Cu, 10 Zn, 1.5 Su
Brass castings, common	20 Cu, 1.25 Zn, 2.5 Su
Brass castings, hard	25 Cu, 2 Zn, 4.5 Su
Brass, propellers	8 Cu, 5 Zn, 1 Su
Gun metal	8 Cu, 1 Su
Copper flanges	9 Cu, 1 Zn, .26 Su
Statuary	91.4 Cu, 5.53 Zn, 1.7 Su, 1.37 Pb
German Silver	2 Cu, 7.9 Ni, 6.3 Zn, 6.5 Fe
Britannia	50 Sb, 25 Su, 25 Bi
Chinese Silver	65.1 Cu, 19.3 Zn, 13 Ni, 2.58 Ag, 12 Fe
Chinese white copper	20.2 Cu, 12.7 Zn, 1.3 Su, 15.8 Ni
Medals	100 Cu, 8 Zn
Babbitt's metal	25 Su, 2 Sb, .5 Cu
Bell metal, large	3 Cu, 1 Su
Bell metal, small	4 Cu, 1 Su
Chinese Gongs	40.5 Cu, 9.2 Su
Telescope mirrors	33.3 Cu, 16.7 Su
White metal, ordinary	3.7 Cu, 3.7 Zn, 14.2 Su, 28.4 Sb
White metal, hard	35 Cu, 13 Zn, 2.2 Su
Metal, expands in cooling	75 Pb, 16.7 Sb, 8.3 Bi

Aluminum.

Although aluminum is one of the most abundant and widely distributed metals, it never occurs free in nature. Our common clay consists chiefly of aluminum silicate and it has been estimated, there is enough aluminum in every brick to form a coating an eighth of an inch thick, over its surface. Therefore it is not the scarcity of aluminum that contributes to its cost; but the expense of extracting it from the silicate.

The only process used at present for the extraction of aluminum is an electrolytic one The apparatus consists of a rectangular iron box, lined with a thick layer of carbon which constitutes the cathode. The inside dimensions are about 4½ feet long, 2½ feet wide, and 6 inches deep. Carbon rods about 3 inches in diameter and 18 inches long, placed in rows and supported by copper bars, serve as the anodes. The process is made continuous by adding raw material at the top and drawing off the aluminum at the bottom. The product is 99 to 99½ per cent pure, and the remaining ½ per cent impurities consists of traces of iron, silicon and sodium. Aluminum melts at 1212 degrees F., and when in the molten state it oxidizes rapidly and absorbs gases.

The strong affinity of aluminum for oxygen is made use of in the product called Thermite.

Thermite.—When a mixture of very fine particles of aluminum and iron oxide (iron rust) is ignited a rapid combustion and very high temperature ensues. In this reaction the oxygen, in the iron oxide, unites with the aluminum, setting the iron free and liberating 4400 degrees heat. This mixture of aluminum and iron oxide is known by the trade name of Thermite, and the reaction of this substance is used to furnish heat and material for *thermite welding.*

CHAPTER V.

ACETYLENE GENERATORS

The function of an acetylene generator, is in principle, a simple one. It has to bring together the water and carbide, wash the gas and store it in such quantities as may be necessary. There are two general methods of bringing the water and carbide together, viz., "carbide to water" and "water to carbide." Generators are therefore more frequently designated as carbide-feed, and water feed, respectively. Inasmuch as it is easier to regulate the flow of water, by means of valves and other methods in common use, than to control the distribution of carbide, it was natural that the earlier generators should operate by sprinkling, or dripping water onto the carbide. Later, it was observed that the more rational plan was to drop suitable quantities of carbide into a large excess of water. From these principles originated the various types of generators which are on the market today.

Recall the heating phenomena of reaction. Water consists of hydrogen and oxygen, the dissociation of which absorbs heat. On the other hand, the oxygen liberated combines with the calcium carbide, and the reaction liberates much more heat than is absorbed by the former reaction. This excess of heat is about 900 B. T. U. per pound of carbide; which is sufficient to raise the temperature of one gallon of water through 90 degrees F. No device or arrangement can alter the amount of heat liberated, and if no cooling is effected, and the carbide is in excess proportion to the water, the temperature may become very high. High temperatures may be caused when large quantities of carbide are heaped in a quantity of water. In the exterior of this heap the water reacts with the carbide rapidly and the heat liberated prevents it reaching the interior of the mass, except in very small quantities. Around the outside the carbide is decomposed to lime, and lime being a poor conductor, prevents the radiation of the heat liberated at the interior. Under these conditions the mixture may become red hot.

Although, as has been said before, no arrangement can alter the amount of heat liberated, the temperature may be regulated by having an excess of water to absorb the heat. Regardless of this there are generators manufactured which do not utilize this or any other cooling agency.

Drip Type Generator.—In this type of generator, small quantities of water are dropped onto a large mass of carbide. The amount of water being regulated by the pressure or quantity of the accumulated gas On account of their simplicity they are frequently used for small portable generators, and when started they should be allowed to work continuously until the supply of carbide is exhausted. These generators give the greatest amount of heating and the most impure gas.

Flooding Type Generators.—In this generator the carbide is placed in pans, having dividing walls to separate them into compartments containing about two pounds each. The water control is arranged to first enter compartment No. 1, exhausts and completely floods it, and then flows into the next compartment where it finds a fresh supply of carbide. This overflowing from one compartment to the other, continues until the contents of the generator are exhausted. These generators possess the same disadvantages as the drip type; but not to so marked a degree.

Carbide to Water Type.—These generators are provided with a hopper of some sort, which contains the carbide, and are provided with a mechanism for automatically dropping it into the water below, at the right time and measured quantities to maintain a constantly uniform pressure. These feeding mechanisms are of two kinds, one consists of some kind of a valve or shutter which opens at the right moment and drops the carbide directly into the water, the other depends on feeding the carbide over the edge of the plate. Either of these arrangements must be safeguarded so that it is impossible to accidently drop the entire quantity of carbide into the water.

The feeding mechanism must be positive, strong and simple, for on it depends the perfect, uninterrupted and economical operation of the machine. It must positively feed carbide when it is needed, and with equal reliability prevent the feeding of

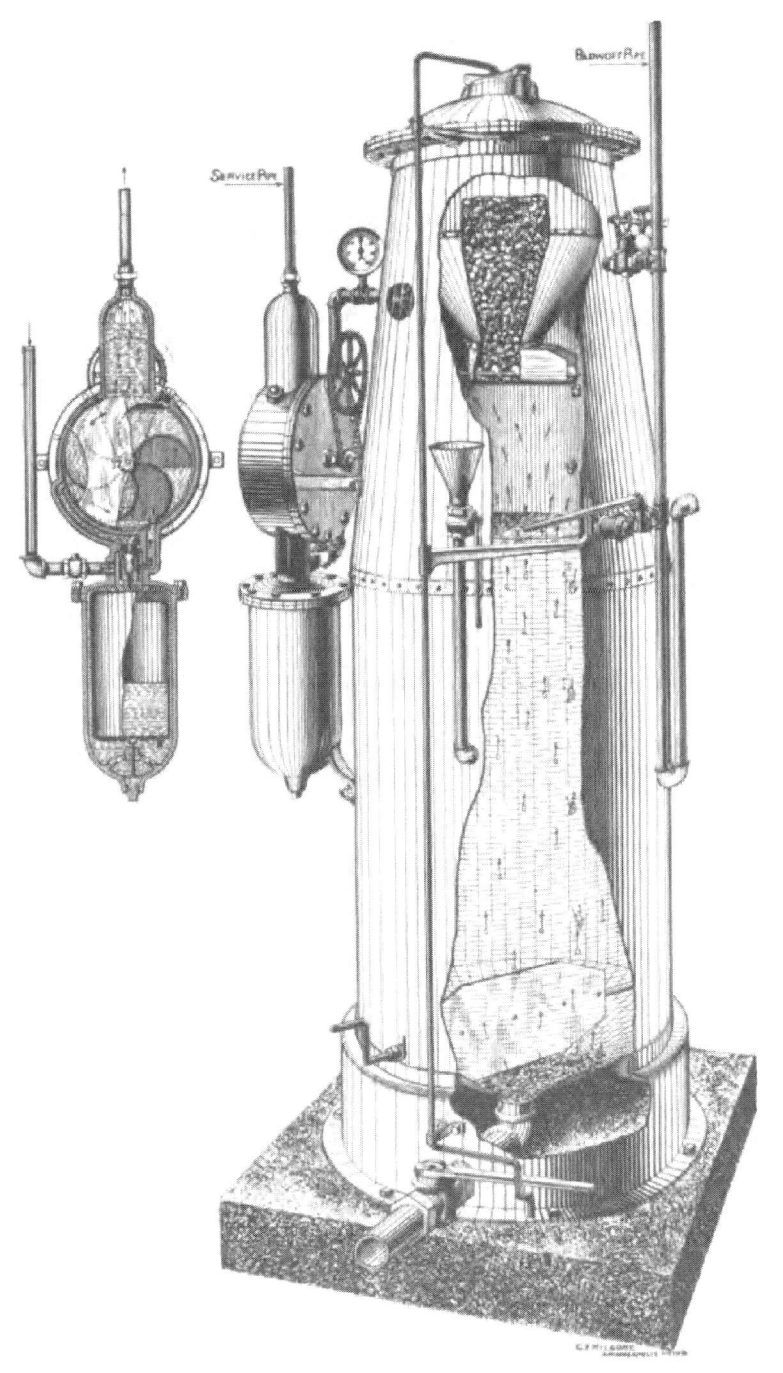

FIG. 14.
TYPICAL CARBIDE TO WATER GENERATOR.

carbide when it is not needed. The water chamber should hold enough water to absorb the heat liberated by the decomposing carbide, without excessive temperature, and the carbide should be fed in very small quantities (piece by piece) with diminishing or increasing frequency as the demand for gas decreases or increases.

When standing in the shop, acetylene generators are subject to accidents and misnaps, just the same as any other piece of equipment; the tang of a file may be thrown through the shell of the generator and allow the gas to escape. To avoid trouble in instances of this nature, the modern generators provide that carbide will not feed into the water in consequence of lowered pressure due to accidents to the generator. This is accomplished by utilizing the flow of gas, to the service pipe, to operate the carbide feed

"Carbide to water" generators as just described, generate the most pure, cool, gas at a constantly uniform pressure. They are more economical, safer, and otherwise more satisfactory than either the Drip Type or Flooding Type generators.

There are two different designs in this type of generator. One having a gasometer in which a quantity of gas is stored ready for instant use; and the other in which no gasometer is required, the gas being generated on demand. Generators without gasometers have the advantage of having less gas in storage in case of injury from accidental causes; they are less liable to give trouble by freezing, they are not so cumbersome to handle and consequently better adapted to portable use.

Selecting a Generator.—As to the selection of a generator, there are good generators in both of the last named types, and it is an easy matter to select the one best suited to your requirements. Of whatever type it may be, a good generator should possess the following qualities·

(1) It must insure cool generation. Since all machines are slightly heated during rapid generation, a pound of carbide decomposed in water always liberates the same amount of heat Nine hundred B. T. U's. are liberated from every pound of

decomposed carbide, and this heat should be absorbed in a sufficient quantity of water to insure that no part will become heated enough to become dangerous.

(2) There should always maintain a constant uniform pressure, sufficient to insure a rapid flow of gas to the torch; but never more than 29 pounds. A pressure of 29 pounds at any point may become a source of danger and more than 15 pounds is unnecessary.

(3) It should be well constructed, built of good material selected to resist the chemical action of the gases and carbide, of sufficient weight and proportion to withstand the stress of careless handling. It should be built for service, and not merely to sell.

(4) It must be simple. Void of numerous or complicated mechanisms, easy to clean and recharge, and reliably automatic in operation.

(5) It should generate the maximum amount of clean washed gas.

(6) It must be so designed, that if any part fails to work, becomes broken or dislodged, it will result in stopping the carbide feed.

(7) The feed regulator should be actuated by the combined influences of lowering pressure and flow of gas to the service pipe; and should not be actuated by either one of these influences alone.

(8) It should be equipped with pressure gauge, safety valve, and an interlocking arrangement of the valve handles that will preclude the possibility of careless manipulation. In other words it should be "fool proof."

Generators of the carbide to water type are undoubtedly the best. With the water in excess, it is impossible for the temperature to rise to the boiling point of water, and under all conditions this class of generator yields the purest gas. As the acetylene bubbles up through the water it is washed free from

ACETYLENE GENERATORS 49

most of its impurities. They are perfectly safe to move on trucks while charged, and under pressure and it is impossible for them to explode if they are designed and constructed on the lines prescribed.

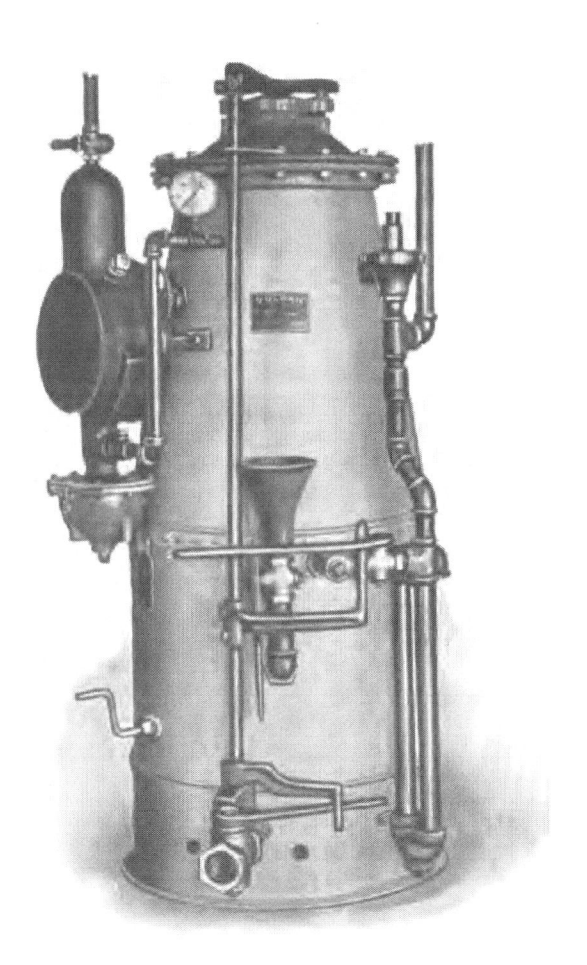

MODERN ACETYLENE GENERATOR

CHAPTER VI.
OXY-ACETYLENE TORCHES.

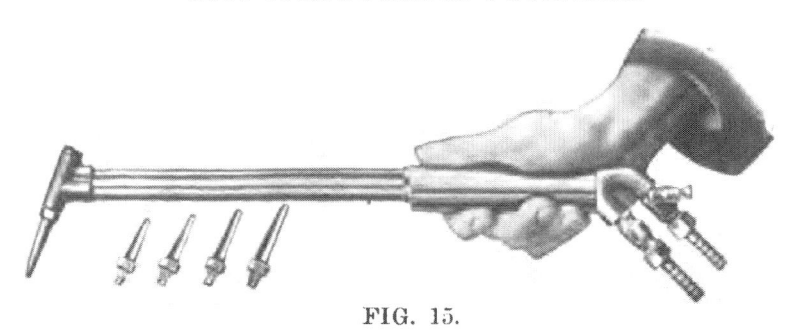

FIG. 15.

MODERN OXY-ACETYLENE WELDING TORCH

To the casual observer, the oxy-acetylene torch is comparatively a simple construction consisting of a body or handle at one end and a mixing head at the other end, equipped with tips or nozzles of various sizes to direct the flame against the work; but the requirements of this torch are very exacting.

The velocity of propagation of the oxy-acetylene flame is about 330 feet per second, and to prevent the flame flashing back into the torch head, it is necessary that the velocity of the gases, as they leave the torch, should equal or exceed this velocity. This "flashing back" is a condition in which the flame enters the end of the torch and follows back into the mixing chamber. This feature in a torch is very annoying and causes much delay, for it necessitates turning off the gases, relighting the torch, and adjusting the flame, before proceeding. While this is being done the work is cooling, thus the delay and inconvenience amounts to more than merely relighting and adjusting the torch.

Acetylene when burned in the air requires about five times its volume of oxygen to completely consume it. This is also true when burning acetylene with the oxy-acetylene torch; but to obtain the best results, it is necessary to only supply one volume of oxygen to one volume of acetylene, the other four volumes of oxygen being supplied by the air. If more or less than one volume of oxygen is delivered by the torch, it results in waste of oxygen, or lowering temperature.

The intense heat obtainable with this torch is dependent on the rapidity of combustion and this, in turn, depends on the thorough mingling of the gases, so that each atom of oxygen is in close association with a molecule of acetylene, ready for instant combination.

To obtain this thorough mixture of equal quantities of gas and eject them at the required velocity, is more difficult to accomplish than might be supposed The factors that contribute to this difficulty are, the difference in specific gravity of the gases, the different pressures at which they are supplied, and the varying quantities required by the different tips

Another feature to be obtained in a good torch, is that it should handle well, or be well balanced to facilitate easy and rapid manipulation. When the torch is being used for welding it is in constant motion, describing little circles of uniform size overlapping each other and equally spaced along the line of the weld. The motion is somewhat similar to that of the penman writing a series of overlapping loops in a continuous uninterrupted line. The reader has perhaps practiced this exercise in penmanship, and knows the importance in having a pen that handles right. A well balanced torch is of equal necessity to the welder.

The foregoing requirements are general and apply to torches of either the high or low pressure types.

According to the pressure of the acetylene supply, oxy-acetylene torches are of two types, the low pressure torch, which is designed to use acetylene at a tension of only a few ounces, and the high pressure torch designed to receive acetylene at a pressure ranging from 2 to 12 pounds.

Low Pressure Torches:—To obtain the desired velocity at the tip of the torch, the oxygen must be delivered at high pressure, and to provide equal volumes of gases, at such a difference in pressure, it is necessary to utilize the velocity of the oxygen to promote the flow of acetylene. This is accomlished by a device similar to the injector, or aspirator. The oxygen nozzle opens into the center of a conical chamber, where it draws in the acetylene, mixes, and is then ejected through an expansion chamber where the velocity is reduced to a suitable value.

The oxygen being supplied at a pressure so greatly in excess to that of the acetylene, it is thought possible for it to blow back through the acetylene tubes, and produce in them a combustible mixture, in fact the first inventors of low pressure torches greatly feared the "flashing back" of the flame into the acetylene pipes, and to prevent this they devised many ingenious arrangements, which are still indispensable.

High Pressure Torches:—The design of high pressure torch is, in a general way, on the same lines of the low pressure torch. That is the injector principle is used; but not to so great an extent

The acetylene and oxygen being used at nearly the same pressure, there is no tendency for the oxygen to blow back into the acetylene tube. A more perfect mixture of gases is obtained, because the oxygen does not tend to force a passage way through the acetylene; but remains in association with it long enough to become thoroughly mingled. This results in greater economy.

The high pressure torch is more universal in application, because flames of different magnitude are obtainable by regulating the valves which control the gas supply, while with the low pressure it is necessary to change the nozzles and mixing chambers. In consequence of these advantages there is a growing favor for high pressure torches.

To facilitate welding in inaccessible places and permit their use in welding machines, high pressure torches are constructed in a variety of lengths and shapes, a few of which are illustrated Fig. 15 shows a torch designed for general hand use. It is provided with "tips" or nozzles of different sizes, and by inserting one or the other, as the occasion may require, the widest range of work may be handled, varying from the thinnest sheet iron to the heaviest steel casting. Table XI, in the back of this volume, gives the size of tip best suited to the weight of the metal being welded, and shows the amount of gases each tip will consume per hour.

When large castings have been preheated to considerable extent, the heat which they radiate to the atmosphere, makes it very uncomfortable for the welder to stand over them and use

ACETYLENE TORCHES

FIG. 16.
OXY-ACETYLENE TORCH

This torch is made longer than the standard, to facilitate welding in places the operator cannot approach on account of inacessibility or radiating heat.

the torch. In these instances it is sometimes more convenient to use a torch of unusual length, so that the welder may stand at a more comfortable distance. These long torches are frequently used to reach a weld that is impossible for the welder to approach on account of it being inaccessible. These torches may be made any length to suit the welder or the occasion, but experience has demonstrated that when the length exceeds 36" the torch becomes difficult to handle On this account, torches for this purpose are usually made about 34" long.

All of the standard torches are constructed to direct the flame down at a right angle to the handle, or at an angle varying lightly from this position. This arrangement makes it impossible to do welding in the bottom of a tank which is too small for the welder to enter, and to facilitate work of this kind, the manufacturers have provided, what might be called a *Straight Line Torch*. In this torch the head and mixing chamber are arranged to deliver the flame straight away from the operator, or in a line with the handle.

Cutting Torches:—Steel plates 1-8 or 3-16 inches thick may be readily cut by the oxy-acetylene process without any special changes in the torches just described, but for greater thicknesses a special torch is required.

FIG. 17.
STRAIGHT LINE TORCH.

A complete description of the oxy-acetylene cutting process is described in chapter XII.

The principle upon which the cutting torch is constructed is to provide a flame to raise the temperature of the metal to redness and then deliver a jet of pure oxygen against the heated surface. Some of the earlier torches resembled the regular welding torch with the addition of an auxiliary oxygen tube. This tube received its supply of oxygen from a point in the handle beyond the control of the needle valves which regulate the flame; and delivered its oxygen close beside the base of the flame.

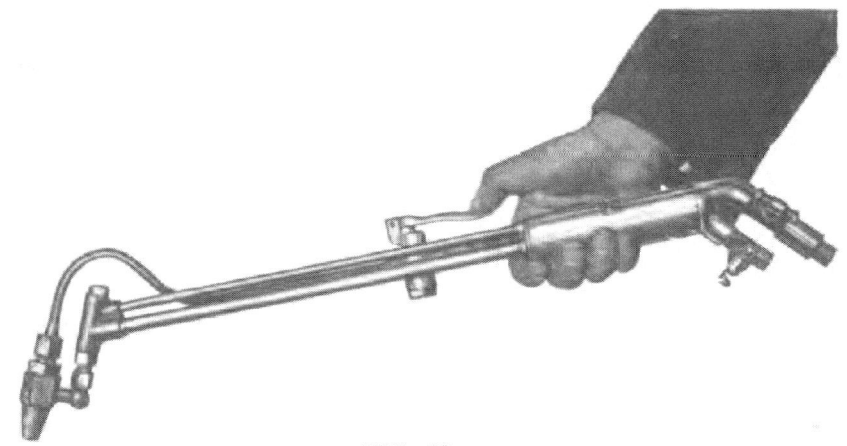

FIG. 18.
OXY-ACETYLENE CUTTING TORCH.

It is provided with a valve to regulate the flow of oxygen, independent of the supply required by the preheating flame.

There are several features, of this type of torch, that are well to consider. The greatest economy and speed are obtained with the purest oxygen. In fact there is considerable effort expended in generating and maintaining pure oxygen for this purpose; but in torches of this type, if the oxygen is polluted with air just at the moment it is to be used, the results are not as satisfactory as they might have been, if the jet of oxygen had been protected from the atmosphere.

Since the preheating flame must precede the oxygen jet in the line of the cut, it follows that these torches can only be advanced in one direction, that is, with the oxygen jet following

ACETYLENE TORCHES

the flame. Then, to cut a hole through a plate, the operator would have to take different positions around the plate. In other words he would either have to walk around his work or assume some exceedingly awkward positions to keep the oxygen jet continually in the rear of the preheating flame

Manufacturers of modern torches have overcome these difficulties by placing the oxygen jet inside of the heating flame. where it is protected from the surrounding air, and is ever in a position to do its work, irrespective of the direction the torch is being moved.

When the occasions for using the cutting torch are frequent and interrupted, it is desirable to possess a torch designed exclusively for this purpose; but if the events of its use are only incidental, an attachment may be applied to the welding torch, which will admirably serve the purpose of the cutting torch, and give as perfect satisfaction.

One or these attachments is illustrated in Fig. 19 which shows the Vulcan Combination Cutting and Welding Torch. This combination consists of an auxiliary oxygen tube and cutting head, which, when attached to the Vulcan welding torch, makes a perfect cutting torch of the modern type, the preheating flame is formed in a hollow annular cone, with the oxygen cutting jet in its center, as described in a previous paragraph.

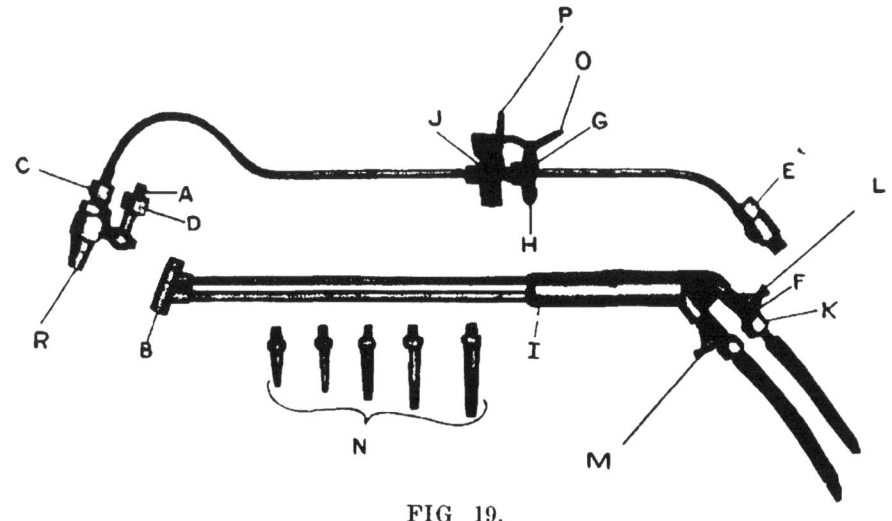

FIG 19.
VULCAN COMBINATION CUTTING AND WELDING TORCH.

Instructions on Assembling Vulcan combination and welding torches are furnished assembled and ready to use, but when a customer has previously purchased a welding torch, and at a later period orders a cutting attachment, he may require some instructions on how to assemble the combination.

Assembling these parts is only the work of a very few moments, and if the same routine is followed each time, the performance becomes habitual, and the combination is made very quickly, without distracting the operator's attention from other work An outline of procedure is recommended as follows, the parts and letters referred to are indicated in Fig. 19.

To quickly assemble this combination, unscrew the union nut C and remove the cutting head from the tube.

Then attach cutting head to the head of the torch by screwing A into B up to the shoulder on A, and tighten by hand. If the cutting head does not align with the torch it should be made to do so, by loosening the nut D and swinging it to the position shown in the illustration. When this position has been obtained the nut D must be screwed down tight onto the cutting head.

The small machine screw H should then be removed from the clamp G and the clamp slipped over the handle on the torch at I

Attach E to F and attach the tube to the cutting head by returning the union nut C to its original position shown in the illustration. Then replace and tighten the machine screw H.

See that the thumb lever O is up in the released position, which closes the oxygen valve J, and close the needle valves L and M.

The torch is now ready to be connected with the hose. Attach the red acetylene hose to the lower connection and the black oxygen hose to the recently applied upper connection.

The oxygen and acetylene gases are ignited at R and the tips N are not used in cutting.

ACETYLENE TORCHES

To remove the cutting attachment, disconnect the oxygen hose, remove machine screw H, disconnect E and C and remove the oxygen tube by slipping clamp G from the handle of the torch; then unscrew A from B, attach the black oxygen hose to the upper connection K, select a tip from N and insert it into B. The torch is then ready to use for welding

Figure 18 shows the complete combination torch.

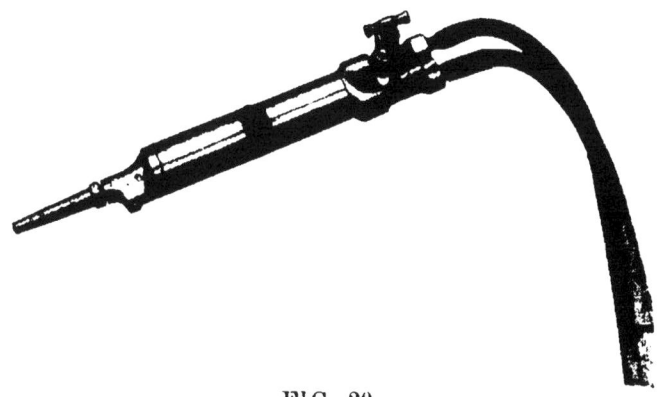

FIG. 20

TORCH DESIGNED FOR WELDING MACHINES.

CHAPTER 7.

PRESSURE REGULATORS.

When oxygen or acetylene is obtained in drums at pressures ranging between 150 and 1,800 per square inch and used at the torch at pressures ranging from 1 to 54 pounds, it becomes necessary to employ some automatic mechanism that will make this reduction, and maintain a constant uniform pressure at the torch, irrespective of the original and constantly diminishing pressure in the drums.

The device used to perform this work, is known among welders as an automatic regulator and accomplishes this regulated pressure reduction by automatically throttling the gas supply so that the pressure will remain uniform at the torch. As the gas enters the regulator it passes through a valve into an expansion chamber, one side of which is a flexible diaphragm. If the quantity of gas entering this expansion chamber exceeds the quantity going out to the torch, there will be a natural tendency to increase the pressure, but this increasing pressure, deflects the diaphragm and partially closes the valve; thus the gas is admitted or throttled to suit the increasing or diminishing demand at the torch.

Fig. 21
AUTOMATIC ACETYLENE REGULATOR

PRESSURE REGULATORS

These regulators are provided with a spring and adjusting screw arranged to bear directly on the diaphragm, so that the final pressure may be adjusted to suit the requirements of the work.

Fig. 22
AUTOMATIC OXYGEN REGULATOR

They are usually provided with one or two gauges to indicate the pressures in the drum and at the torch.

A low pressure regulator equipped with one indicator is shown in Figure 21. The indicator dial shows the pressure of gas going to the torch, and the T handle on the front is used to adjust this pressure as the requirements demand.

This type regulator is usually used on acetylene generators, because in this service it is only required to know the pressure of the gas going to the torch, the pressure in the generator being indicated by an independent gauge.

60 OXY-ACETYLENE WELDING AND CUTTING

A high pressure regulator with two indicators is shown in Figure 22. One indicator shows the pressure in the drum, and the other the pressure of the gas going to the torch. When used on oxygen drums the high pressure indicator is useful in determining the amount of gas in the drum as explained on page 26. it is therefore, sometimes called an *Oxygen Regulator*.

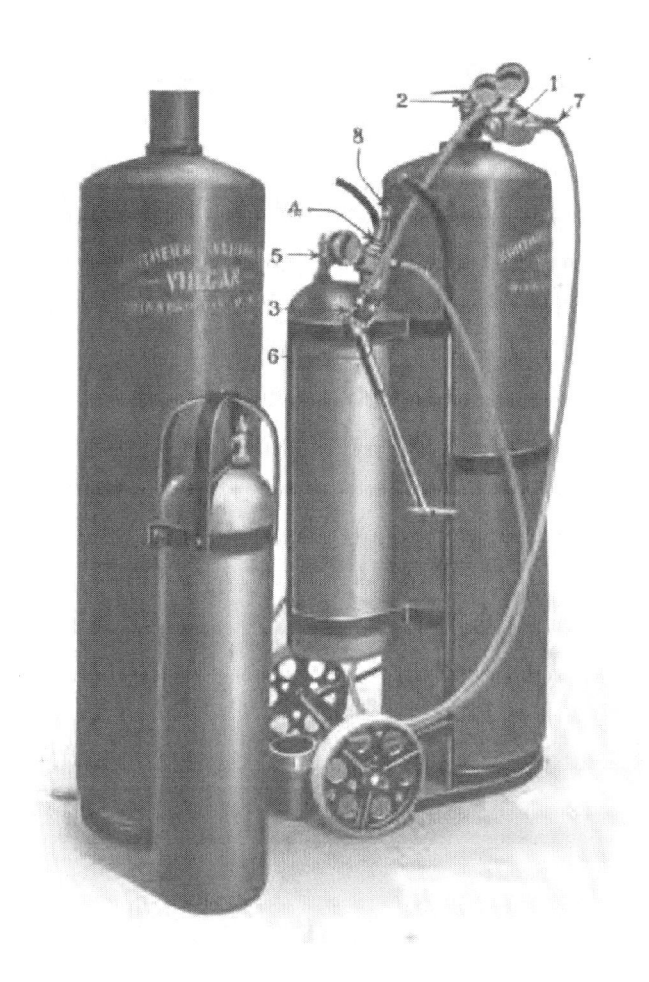

Fig. 23
OXY-ACETYLENE WELDING PLANT
Showing application of automatic pressure regulators

CHAPTER 8.

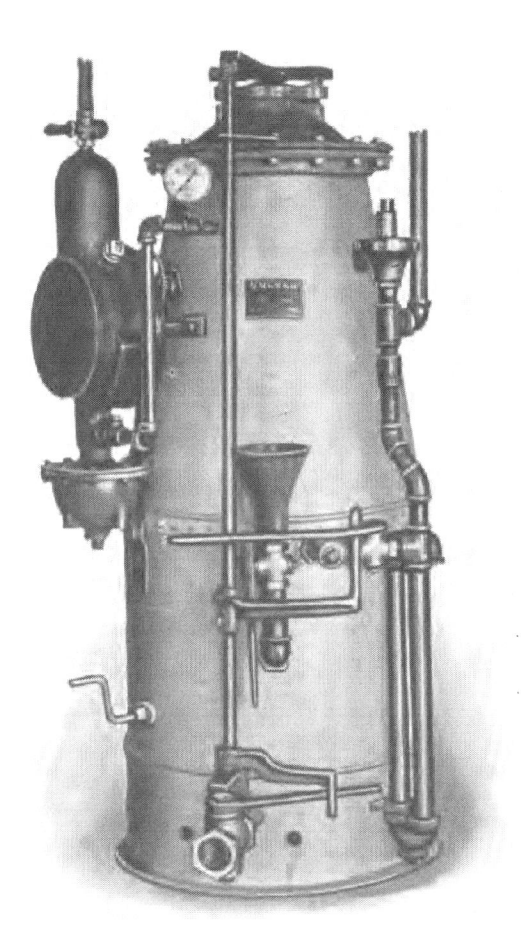

Fig. 30
VULCAN AUTOMATIC ACETYLENE GENERATOR

Chapter five outlines the various types of generators that can be used to produce acetylene gas. In reading over the advantages and disadvantages of the different methods of generating acetylene, it will be noted that the "carbide to water feed" generator has none of the disadvantages of the other types, but does have a great many advantages that are not possessed by the others.

Of the two styles of generators, low and medium pressure, the latter is the better for welding, because the acetylene and oxygen, should be delivered to the mixing chamber of the welding torch at as near the same pressure as can be secured.

Where both gases are thus combined under positive, even pressure their mixture is more complete—assuming that the mixing chamber of the torch is properly constructed. Unless this thorough mixing of the two gases takes place, the result will be incomplete combustion, hence waste of gas and loss in efficiency.

With the low pressure or gasometer type of generators, the injector type of torch is principally used. By this is meant that oxygen under high pressure, in passing through the mixing chamber of the torch, sucks the acetylene through with it. In this way the two gases are not thoroughly mixed, and the result is a waste of gas and a poor weld. The feeding mechanism of most pressure generators, now on the market, are operated by means of complicated clock-work with pulleys and weights, leather diaphragms, etc. These frequently get out of order at just the time when operator needs the gas the most and the resulting delays are expensive as well as annoying.

The *Vulcan* automatic acetylene generator works on entirely new principles, and the features that contribute to its success are so simple, unique, and perform their duty so accurately that the generator is well worth consideration.

Its design is such that the demand for gas or the flow of gas to the service pipe, working in conjunction with the amount of pressure in the generator, automatically regulates the gas generation to meet the varying demand at a uniform pressure. The rate at which the carbide is fed into the water varies directly with the rate at which the gas is used, and no more carbide is fed than is absolutely necessary to maintain the pressure at that particular moment. If gas is being used and pressure up to normal, or vice-versa if the gas is not being used but the pressure below normal, the carbide feed is inactive; but under these conditions a very slight drop in pressure, or the renewed demand for gas will cause the right amount of generation to take care of the moment's demand.

The carbide feed automatically drops small quantities of $1\frac{1}{4}$ x$\frac{3}{8}$ carbide, deep into a liberal quantity of water, and as the gas bubbles rise to the surface, they are cooled and washed, and emerge free from dust or other impurities.

By the arrangements set forth, many advantages are obtained.

The most apparent of which is a very constant uniform pressure. After generation is eliminated on account of there being only a very small quantity of carbide dropped at one time, and the gases are cool because there is not sufficient reaction taking place to perceptibly raise the temperature of the large volume of water. The 1¼x⅜ carbide used in this machine generates one half a cubic foot more gas per pound, than the quarter or finely crushed carbide, and since all sizes of carbide are retailed at the same price this feature alone effects a saving of 12½ per cent in the cost of generation. The motor that operates the carbide feed is imposed between the generating chamber and the service pipe, and for the reason that it is not operated by the deminishing gas pressure only, but by the flow of gas to the service pipe combined with reducing pressure, the arrangement is an assurance that all the carbide will not be fed, or an excessive amount of gas generated, should the gas holder be accidentally punctured. The last mentioned, is a common fault of generators actuated by reduced gas pressure only.

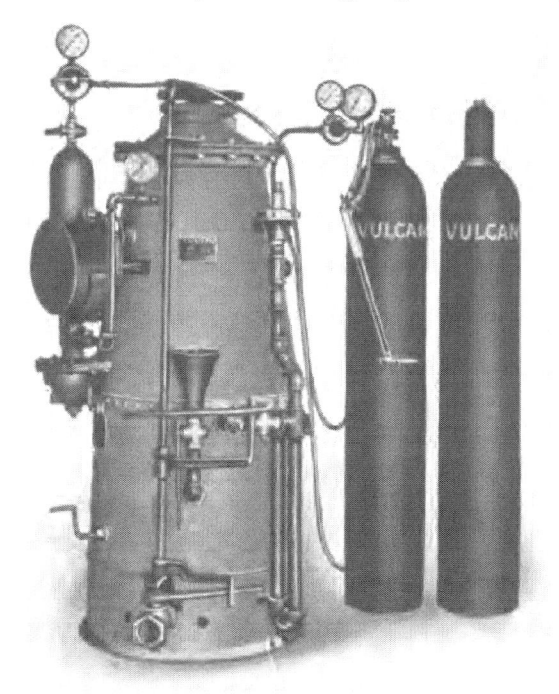

Fig. 31
VULCAN GENERATOR WELDING PLANT

A word about the unique features of the motor will interest the reader. The runner or wheel from which power is received is entirely incased and not visible, but when removed it resembles an old-fashioned over-shot water-wheel. With the water-wheel power is derived from the weight of the water, in the buckets, descending and rotating the wheel; but the wheel of the Vulcan motor is submerged in water and operated by the buoyancy of the gas gathering under the inverted concave buckets and rotating the wheel, in its ascent from the generating chamber to the service pipe The arrangement is such that if the pressure is up to normal, the gas is diverted through a by-pass, to the service pipe, without rotating the motor.

In this description the reader will note the absence of springs, clock-work or weights which might make the apparatus cumbersome.

The generator is designed to deliver gas, at twelve pounds pressure, to oxy-acetylene welding and cutting torches. The pressure selected is deemed most suitable for the work.

The suggestions and rules of the consulting engineers of the National Board of Fire Underwriters are strictly followed, in the manufacture and construction of Vulcan Acetylene Generators, and every precaution has been taken to insure safety and efficiency. The materials are the best, the proportions ample, and the workmanship accurate, so that with proper handling the operation will be eminently successful. To insure that these generators will be properly handled by even the most careless operators, each generator is equipped with a system of guards so interlocked that it is impossible for an absent-minded operator to make mistakes. In fact there is only one way they can be manipulated, and that is the right way. Although it is impossible to pursue wrong methods in operating this plant we will outline the proper method. In this outline the parts referred to are indicated in Figure 32.

Pipe No. 1 is the blow-off and should be extended, without traps and as few elbows as possible, to the outside of the building, and the end pointed down to exclude snow, birds, etc. Pipe No 2 is the service pipe and, if the shop is piped, it should be connected to the supply line, but if it is intended to use gas directly from the generator, though the hose, connect pipe No. 2 with the acetylene regulator.

Fill the chamber No. 3 and motor case No. 4 with water through hole No. 5 and allow to stand a few minutes for air bubbles to work out.

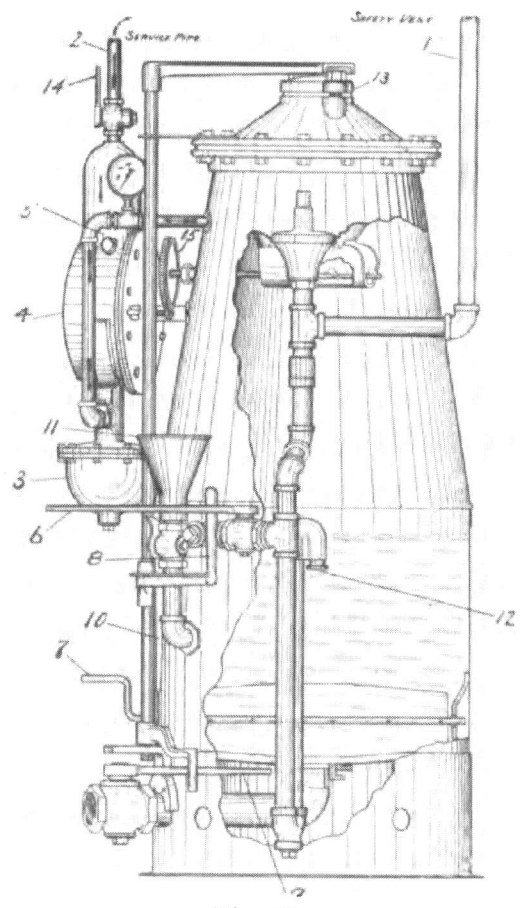

Fig. 32
INTERIOR OF VULCAN GENERATOR

Before replacing the plug into No. 5 be sure the motor case is filled to overflowing.

To charge, or recharge the generator relieve the pressure by turning lever No. 6 one-quarter turn to the right, then agitate the sediment so it will run out, by rotating the crank No. 7. Open the locking device by turning handle No. 8 one-quarter turn to the left. Draw off the sediment through sludge cock by turning handle No. 9 one-quarter turn to the left. After draining, close sludge cock before proceeding further.

Now swing lever No. 10 to a horizontal position and fill the lower part of the generator with water through funnel No. 11 until it overflows through No. 12; then return handle to No 10 to its original vertical position. Remove cover No. 13, fill the carbide hopper with 1¼x⅜ carbide, replace cover and tighten cap screws even and equally. Lock up the generator by swinging lever No. 8 to the right in its original position and closing lever No. 6 to the left over it. Put valve handle No. 14 in a vertical position which closes the service cock.

The generator is now ready for pressure which is started by rotating gear wheel No. 15 to the left until the pressure gauge indicates about three pounds. The carbide will then feed automatically and the pressure rise to the proper amount as soon as the service cock is opened and a little gas drawn off through the torch.

From this on the Vulcan Generator is entirely automatic and needs no further attention until the contents are entirely exhausted.

On account of these generators being self contained, compact in form, and complete without the necessity of a cumbersome gasometer, they are very suitable for portable purposes.

One of these generators mounted on a truck, with oxygen drums and tool box, is shown in Figure 33. This makes a complete portable plant which may be taken to the work anywhere about the shop or yards.

Vulcan Generators are Safe because there is less surface subjected to injury than in many other types.

There are no pipe connections between widely separated parts

They are less liable to freeze than generators having gasometers

Every movable part is safe guarded in a way that makes them fool proof.

The carbide charge cannot be accidentally discharged into the water.

It cannot be overfilled with water.

Fig. 33
VULCAN PORTABLE GENERATOR PLANT

CHAPTER 9.

OPERATING PLANTS.

This might be more correctly called operating a welding shop, for it is the writer's intention to call attention to a few of the essential details, both in equipping and operating a shop. The subject covers such a range of information, that it would be impossible to mention every detail, in fact it would not be practical to undertake such a task, for the equipment will be great or small, according to the amount and nature of the work which the operator expects to provide for.

Whether the amount of work is considerable or not, there is one thing that should be uppermost in the mind of the operator, that is thoroughness and excellency of work. No matter how small or how large the job, the welding should be thoroughly, carefully and conscientiously performed. After a job has been finished it is often difficult to determine whether it is well done or not, this information may only be obtained by observing the welder while he is doing his work or testing the weld after it has been finished. Sometimes it is impractical to do either of these, and the integrity of the welder must be relied upon.

Recognizing this truth, it is often the practice of boiler inspectors, to condemn any welding on boilers which has not been done by welders of "known reputation," and since boiler work covers a large per cent of the field of his usefulness, the welder should make every effort to get into the class of welders of "known reputation." This also applies to other kinds of work. The occasions that require autogenous welding are frequently of great importance. It may be a crank shaft or cylinder for some power plant, and if the welder does his work thoroughly, the job will hold and be as good as a new piece; but if he is hasty or careless it will be very liable to fail, resulting in loss of time, money and possibly loss of life. For this reason persons who have work of this kind are wont to patronize welders of "known reputation."

In work of the kind just described, the saving in time and money is sufficient to pay the welder handsomely for all the time, care, or expense he may devote to thoroughly doing his work and there is no excuse for slighting the job on the pretext that his customer will object to the expense. The only complaint that could justly be made, would be for time covered by idleness, for lack of foresight that may cause loss of time or delay, or charging for a service which you are not equipped to render.

Any equipment the welder can provide, will lessen the cost of the work and often facilitate better work. Therefore equipment sufficient for the work you expect to handle is an asset, which can hardly be dispensed with. Such conveniences as an assortment of handy tools arranged within easy reach, benches, brick welding tables, preheating furnaces, and facilities for handling heavy work, contribute to good service and the pleasure of work, and are conveniences that may be built and installed during ones spare moments.

Many welders have started their plant in a very modest way, buying their gases in drums and in every way curtailing the amount of the original investment. As their business grew their mind was occupied in pursuing their trade, and the fact that their acetylene was costing them more than twice as much as it should, did not occur to them until they learned that a competitor charged one cent a foot for acetylene and made profit on it; whereas he could not make a profit on acetylene at 2 1-4c a foot. This leads to the explanation that acetylene in drums has an economic place in plants that have to be quickly transported to some remote location, over rough roads, in cold weather and also in shops where the occasions for using the apparatus are not very frequent. The cost of acteylene in drums is 2c per foot at the recharging station and to this cost is added freight and cartage, while the cost of acetylene generated on the premises of the welding shop, seldom exceeds 7-8c per foot. In a shop where the welder uses the torch 6 hours a day, the saving effected, by generating his own acetylene, will amount to $2.50 or $3.00 per day.

In shops that are provided with an acetylene generator it is advisable to give it a permanent location in some corner where it will be out of the way and protected against freezing.

The advantages of a permanent location for the generator are many. The time used in trucking it around the shops is eliminated, the blow off and sludge pipes can be extended to outside the building, water may be piped to a place convenient to the generator, the generator will be less liable to become injured by collision, and the acetylene may be piped to any part of the building with drops and hose connections at different places most convenient to the work.

Piping:—Acetylene generators are usually regulated to control the gas pressure at about 12½ pounds per square inch and since the largest tips consume gas at very nearly this pressure, it is essential that the gas should be conveyed through the pipes with as little loss of pressure as possible. It is recommended that the loss of pressure should not exceed 8 ounces. The factors to be considered in determining the loss in pressure are, the length and diameter of the pipe, the specific gravity and the initial and final pressures of the gas. The quantity of acetylene which will be delivered through pipes of different sizes with a loss in pressure of 8 ounces from an initial pressure of 11½ pounds, may be calculated from the following formula, in which (D) represents the inside diameter of the pipe in inches and (L) its length in feet.

$$2809\sqrt{\frac{26\ D^5}{L}} \quad \text{quanty of gas.}$$

TABLE IX.

ACETYLENE DELIVERED BY PIPES OF VARIOUS SIZES AND LENGTHS, WITH LOSS OF 8oz. PRESSURE FROM AN INITIAL PRESSURE OF 11½ LBS.

Nominal Size of Pipe	\multicolumn{7}{c}{Length of Pipe in feet}
	100	200	300	400	500	600	700
½	434	306	250	216	193	177	163
¾	872	616	503	436	390	356	329
1	1,618	1,144	934	809	723	660	611
1¼	3,204	2,266	1,850	1,602	1,433	1,308	1,211

In using this table the pipe fitter should add to the actual length of the pipe, a sufficient length to compensate for the fittings, as obtained from table VIII.

The effect of a bend or sharp angle in a pipe is to retard the flow of gas. This is least when the radius of the bend is five times the radius of the pipe. The most convenient way of stating the resistance offered by bends, is in terms of equivalent length of straight pipe which offers the same resistance to the flow as the extra resistance due to the bend. A formula given for this equivalent length is

$$L = 12.85 \left(\frac{r}{R}\right)^{.83} l$$

L=equivalent in feet

r=radius of pipe

R=radius of curve

l=length of curve in feet measured on center line.

The following table gives the additional length required to equal the friction due to globe valves. For standard elbows and trees, take ⅔ the value given in the table.

TABLE VIII.

ADDITIONAL LENGTHS OF PIPE THAT WILL CAUSE FRICTION EQUAL TO THE FRICTION DUE TO GLOBE VALVES.

Diameter of pipe in inches.	Additional length in feet.
1	2
1½	4
2	7
2½	10
3	13
3½	16
4	20
5	28
6	36

The blow-off or exhaust pipe should extend to the outside of the building with as few elbows as possible and terminate with the end pointing down to exclude the snow and water.

The sludge pipe or drain pipe as it is commonly called should not lead direct to a sewer, but should first discharge into an open pit. This pit may be provided with an overflow, about 3 feet above the bottom, which may then lead to a sewer. The pipes from the generator to the pit should have a fall of about one inch to twelve feet and from the pit to the sewer one inch to 20 feet. If a sludge pit is constructed that will drain and leave the residuum comparatively dry, this material may become of some pecuniary value. The chief uses of the sludge, frequently called acetylene lime, are for mixing mortar, for whitewashing fences, cattle pens, fruit trees, etc., for making paths, and for fertilizing, with some occasional application as an insecticide and disinfectant, mortar made from it is reported to bind quickly and hard; there is no reason why mortar made from it should not be at least of equal value with mortar made from slaked lime. It may be added that any of the uses to which ordinary lime white wash is applied, a white wash made of carbide residuum answers equally as well.

In view of the many particular uses to which acetylene lime has been successfully applied, and particularly because of its usefulness as a fertilizer, it may not be out of place to submit the chemical analysis of carbide residuum. The following figures show the analysis of three specimens of residue taken at remote places.

	1 Per cent	2 Per cent	3 Per cent
Sand (silica)	1.24	1.10	.97
Carbon (coke or coal)	2.08	3.95	2.14
Oxide of iron and aluminum	3.11	2.9	2.3
Lime	62.5	63.65	66.1
Water and carbonic acid	31.04	28.4	28.47

The services pipes, or mains that connect the generator with the torches must be securely fastened, without sags that may form pockets and when practical, they should drain toward the generator. It is advisable to use galvanized pipe because the acetylene is usually a little moist and forms oxide of iron, which comes off in a powder and may accumulate in certain parts. Pipes of red copper are strictly prohibited because the acetylene and copper can form acetylide of copper, which is spontaneously combustible.

Testing: As soon as the pipes are all in place and are properly secured, the system should be tested, to find whether it is perfectly gas tight. A convenient nipple should be selected for making connection to the proving pump (an ordinary auto pump will do), and every other opening or fitting should be tightly closed. The pump may then be connected and air forced into the system until the pressure gauge registers 14 or 15 pounds. The pump should then be shut off, leaving the gauge under pressure. The extent of the leak may be judged by the rapidity of the fall in pressure; but its location must be found by following the pipe line and listening for the hiss of escaping air and by applying soapy water to the joints, with a heavy brush.

The oxycetylene welding and cutting outfit is the best tool for making the pipe connections, for with it the pipes may be cut to any length, heated for bending, and the joints welded. The welded joints will never leak or give trouble whereas screwed joints might leak.

After the pipes have been thus inspected and proven satisfactory, the pressure may be released, the generator started, and the gas pressure raised to 12 or 13 pounds. After a little gas has been drawn off at the extreme ends of the pipe and its branches, it should be tightly closed and allowed to stand at the pressure stated, for several hours. Then if there are any leaks, their presence will be noted by the smell. A mixture of acetylene and air in the proportion of 1 to 10000 can be clearly detected by the smell. Do not hunt for leaks with a light.

Leaks in The Oxygen Pipes:—Oxygen is an odorless gas and its abundance in the room is neither noticeable nor harmful, but it is certainly not a very economical practice to allow it to escape, although it is not harmful nor explosive it may be a source of danger, if allowed to blow against the clothing while the torch is being used.

If oxygen is blowing against the clothes they are extremely inflammable and will ignite with a small spark from the torch, the flames may extinguish themselves by evading the oxygen, but a bad burn may result before this is done.

Read Instructions:—Carefully read all the instructions attending the apparatus, go over each piece and understand it before attempting to use it. This may save long delays and much correspondence, for it is not an uncommon thing for manufactures of welding apparatus, to receive complaints that the torch would not work, the tips would not fit, or that parts were missing and after long correspondence, learn that the apparatus was all right; but the customer had neglected to read the instructions and did not know how to assemble his equipment.

Welding Table:—Aside from the work benches and tools, one of the first requisites of the welding shop is the welding table. Whenever the work to be welded is not too large or too difficult to manipulate, the operation is best carried out on a table These tables should be entirely of metal except the top which may be made of a good grade of brick, preferably fire brick. The nature of the work to be handled on them, will, of course regulate their size; but a table 4 feet by 6 feet and 24 inches high will be best suited to the average run of work. For light welding on aluminum work they may be made a little higher, 33 inches being a good height. These tables are best built of $2\frac{1}{2}$x$2\frac{1}{2}$x3-16 angles assembled and welded with the torch. The welded joints give the table rigidity and make the beginner familiar with the work. The material required for the table described above would consist of 4 pieces of angle 6 feet long, 4 pieces 4 feet long, 4 pieces 2 feet long, and 7 pieces of lighter material 43 inches long. The 6 and 4 feet lengths are welded together at the corners with one leg of the angle standing vertical and the other projecting inward, making two frames 6 feet by 4 feet out side. One of these frames is used for the table top and the other for a tool tray beneath. The 2 foot lengths are used for legs, fitting the inside of the angle over the corners of the frames and welding them. The bottom of the tool tray should be about 10 in. above the floor and fitted with about 16 gauge steel sheet. The 43 inch lengths will be spaced 9 inches apart and welded between the edges of the angles forming the table top. The top of the horizontal leg of these angles will be flush with the horizontal leg of the angles forming the table top, and the vertical leg will extend below. Their purpose is to support the brick filling, composing the top, and for that reason they should be placed beneath the joints of the brick. Figure 23 shows one of these tables with part of the brick removed to expose their support.

Fig. 23
WELDING TABLE CONSTRUCTED OF ANGLE IRON

On these tables, there can be built, temporary preheating furnaces for heating work preparatory to welding, or they may be designed to include permanent furnaces formed in the brick work of their top. Here is an opportunity for the welder to display his ingenuity in designing a combined table and preheating furnace.

Some manufactures build a combination table, or more correctly, a combination tool consisting of an iron table top with slotted holes for clamping down work, a long V bar, blocks for aligning and welding crank shafts, and a swivel vise for holding irregular shaped pieces. The top portion of the stand incorporates a ball and socket joint, which permits rotating the work or clamping it at any angle that will facilitate easy manipulation. The tool is a great convenience and may be classified among the time saving devices that go to make up an up-to-date shop.

Fig. 24
COMBINATION WELDING TABLE

Preheating Furnaces:—For reasons, which will be described fully under the chapter on welding, any welding shop is incomplete without some provision for preheating and slowly cooling his work. In the absence of a special furnace one should always have the material at hand for building a temporary affair of brick and sheet asbestos. These are very quickly and easily constructed and serve their purpose very well. Even when shops are equipped with permanent preheating furnaces, there will be occasions when special furnaces will be required for special work, and in view of this fact it is well to describe the method of their construction, so the beginning will be prepared when the occasion comes.

Building a Furnace:—The article to be heated is placed on one of the brick topped tables, previously described, and blocked up with brick. Around this is layed a course of brick about six or eight inches away from the article, and placed end to end with a space of about an inch and a half between them. These spaces are for air draft and on rare occasions it may be necessary to remove a brick from the table top, to admit air to the interior. On top of this course are piled other brick, built like a wall to a height a little above the top of the piece to be welded.

The fuel used is charcoal, which is made into an even bed all around and beneath the article. Sheets of ⅛ inch asbestos are layed loosely over the whole furnace and the charcoal ignited through the holes at the bottom of the wall. The article should be arranged so that the part to be welded will be uppermost. Then when the proper temperature has been attained, an opening can be made through the asbestos and the weld finished without removing it from the fire.

Very often gas burners may be procured, from the dealer, which may be connected with the acetylene pipe and found very convenient for preheating. It may be added that burners designed for city gas might not give satisfaction when used with acetylene. If one intends to equip with preheating burners, it is best to procure burners designed for the gas he intends to use.

Protecting Apparatus:—Oxy-actylene cutting and welding apparatus are not classified among the delicate instruments that are liable to become dearranged and out of order; but they deserve and require care.

They are designed to maintain the purity of the gases. To generate cool and commercially pure acetylene at a continually uniform pressure and deliver it to the torch in the same condition. The oxygen is reduced from an extremely high pressure to a very low one and this reduction is regulated to a nicety. The torch mixes these gases in exact proportions and burns them in a small but exceedingly hot flame where the gases are completely burned and none escape unconsumed. The manufacturers of carbide, from which the acetylene is made, exercise the greatest care to secure and use none but the most pure material; and the manufacturers of oxygen struggle to maintain a standard which does not vary three tenths of one percent, from perfectly pure gas.

The manufacturers go to all this trouble because they understand and know that such precautions are necessary to produce the best results in the welding shop, and these details have been mentioned here to admonish the welder to keep his apparatus clean and protect it from harm, for it is not reasonable to presume that good work may be done when the appliances are kept in a careless or slovenly manner.

All acetylene generators use water in their operation and for that reason they must be protected from freezing. The quantity of water is proportioned to the amount of carbide they hold and if the sediment of carbide is allowed to accumulate in the bottom of the generator it reduces the water capacity and causes other irregularities in its operation. It is therefore a good rule to never fill the generator with fresh carbide until after the sludge has been cleaned from the bottom.

Oxygen is stored in the drums under very high pressure, and if this pressure is suddenly admitted into the regulator, it is liable to injure the mechanism of the regulator, or pressure gauges. The valve on top of the oxygen drum should therefore be opened slowly and left wide open while in use.

Fig. 25
OPEN THE VALVE ON THE OXYGEN DRUM SLOWLY

Before opening this valve it is well to have the adjusting screw on the regulator, unscrewed until it is quite free and other valves closed.

There should be some arrangement to securely hold the oxygen drums in an upright position, for on account of their narrow base they may be easily knocked over and in this event the valve is liable to be injured.

Fig. 26
REMOVABLE BASE FOR OXYGEN DRUMS

Some manufacturers provided a removable base which may be applied to oxygen drums to prevent their upsetting. This appliance allows more freedom since the drum is not confined to any particular location for securing, but may be moved about at the welder's convenience.

When welding over a preheating fire, where the article being welded is imbeded in glowing coals, it is good practice to shield the torch from the direct heat of the fire, with sheets of asbestos. The first time the torch is used over the direct flare of the fire there will probably be no perceptible harm done to it; but a repetition of this practice will, in time, damage it.

Flashing Back:—While the torch is overheated in this way it may cause temporary annoyance by flashing back. This annoyance may be removed by cooling the torch in water. If in the course of the work it is desired to cool the torch in this way, the acetylene should be completely shut off and the flow of oxygen reduced to a very small amount. The object in leaving a small flow of oxygen is to prevent water entering the torch, by the eflux of gas from the tip.

The propagation of the oxy-acetylene flame is about 330 feet a second. This is the speed at which a flame will travel through a tube containing a proper mixture of oxygen and acetylene. If the gases are not expelled from the tip of the torch at a speed equal to or greater than this, the flame will follow back through the tip into the chamber where the gases are mixed and the torch is said to "Flash Back." While the gases are burning in the torch, it is not an unusual occurrence to see long, slender, yellow streaks of flame shoot from the tip.

If the torch is permitted to do this frequently, or to continue burning in the head for a short time, it damages it and makes a repetition of this "Flashing Back" more probable. The gases should therefore be turned off immediately, shutting off the oxygen first.

The "Flashing Back" is more usually caused by an insufficient gas pressure, and if both gases are turned on a little stronger, and the flame readjusted to "neutral" the trouble will usually cease; but insufficient pressure is not the only cause which may effect "Flashing Back." If the torch is held close enough to the work to impede the flow of gas, it may "Flash Back;" but in this event, other conditions being normal, it should relight when it is withdrawn. If the tip is mutilated or roughened inside or at the end it may produce eddy-currents that will cause "Flashing Back;" or if the torch is held too close to melted metal, the force of the gas may splash the metal into the tip and produce eddy-currents that will cause the same effect.

Clean Hose—Oxygen will not burn. In the presence of substances containing carbon or hydrogen it may produce flame, but it is the carbon or hydrogen which burns, and the oxygen supports combustion.

If the oxygen hose are allowed to lay around on a floor that is soaked with kerosene or lubricating oil, the oil will creep into the end and when the oxygen is turned on, the hose will be liable to burn. This can cause no further damage than to destroy the hose, for if the oxygen and oxygen drums are pure and clean, the fire can not enter the drum.

Acetylene is a carbonous gas and may leave slight deposits of carbon on the inside of the acetylene regulator and hose. If the acetylene regulator and hose are used in the oxygen service they are liable to be damaged by the combustion of these carbon deposits.

Acetylene In Drums: It has been explained under the chapter on chemistry that acetylene under high pressure might become dangerous to handle; but dissolved acetylene in drums, under pressure, has extended the usefulness of the gas to a wonderful extent. Acetone is a hydro-carbon and the product of distillation of wood. It is a colorless, inflammable fluid and is much used in the manufacture of chloroform, iodoform, and other medical preparations. This long known but rather unfamiliar fluid is an excellent solvent for acetylene, which dissolves in it as freely as sugar does in water. The solubility increases with pressure and at atmospheric temperature and pressure it will dissolve 24 times its bulk of acetylene.

This phenomenon is utilized to the great advantage of the welder by dissolving acetylene in drums of acetone. The drums supplied are 33 inches long by 8 inches in diameter and contain 100 feet of acetylene. They are perfectly safe to handle, convenient for portable purposes, give no trouble by freezing, and the gas is cool, clean and dry. Since the gas issues at a high pressure, it is necessary to employ a regulator to bring it down to the proper working pressure.

Portable Acetylene Drum Plant:—A small but very convenient plant, in which dissolved acetylene is used, is shown in figure No. 27. This plant consists of two drums of oxygen and two of acetylene with the necessary complement of torches, regulators and apparatus to make up a complete outfit. One drum of each gas is mounted on a truck for convenience in moving and the other two drums are used for storage.

The plant is always ready for use and while the acetylene costs a little more than in the generator plants, it is perfectly practical for the man who does only a moderate amount of work.

A paragraph on connecting and operating a plant of this description will not be out of place. The numbers and parts referred to will be found in figure No. 27.

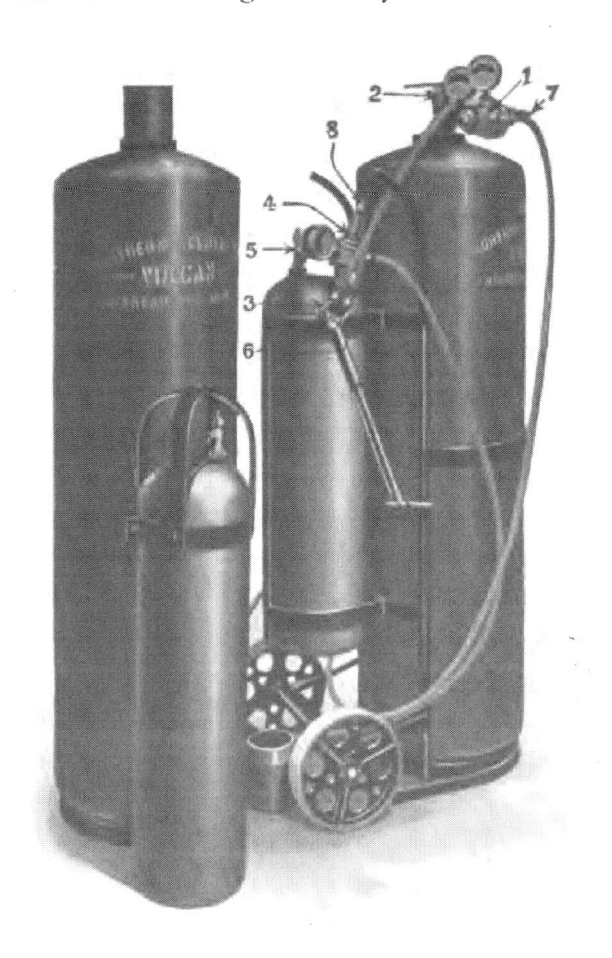

Fig. 27
PORTABLE PLANT USING DISSOLVED ACETYLENE

Connect the oxygen regulator No. 1 to the valve No. 2 on the oxygen drum. Then attach the black oxygen hose to the regulator and the upper valve No. 3 on the torch. Connect the acetylene regulator No. 4 to the valve No. 5 on the acetylene drum. Then attach the red acetylene hose to the regulator and the lower valve on the torch. Unscrew the regular handles Nos. 7 and 8 until they do not bear on the spring inside. This will close the regulators and prevent the passage of gas when the drum valves are opened. Now open the drum valves 2 and 5, and the torch valves 3 and 6. Screw in the handle on the acetylene regulator until the gas begins to flow and adjust the flame, as will be described in Chapter No. 11. The apparatus is now ready to use for welding. When not in use the connections may be left intact with the valves closed.

Portable Acetylene Generator:—A portable generator plant is provided for welders who prefer to take advantage of the saving that may be effected by generating their own acetylene. The plant consists of a generator of 25 or 50 pounds capacity mounted on a four wheeled truck with two oxygen drums and usually provided with a tool box for supplies and small apparatus. One of these plants is shown in figure No. 28. It will be connected and operated much the same as the plant just described except that the acetylene regulator will of course be attached to the generator instead as directed in the previous paragraphs.

Two colored hose are provided to distinguish between the oxygen and acetylene, and it is recommended to use the black hose for the former and the red hose for the latter.

Regulating the Charge For Weldings—Purchasers of welding outfits are immediately confronted with the problem, of how to adjust their charge for services, to conform with the usual practice.

To give explicit directions for making charges would be useless, the location of the plant with references to neighboring towns, shipping facilities, the comparative cost of labor and commodities, the risk attending the work, the urgency of the demand, the cost of a new piece to replace the broken one and the cost of gases including freight and cartage, are all factors to be considered in determining a just charge. A knowledge of how these factors enter into consideration is best conveyed to the beginner by illustrations.

As a rule it is advisable to make a minimum charge, which may range between 75 cents and $1.00. This, however, can not be rigidly adhered to.

Fig. 28
PORTABLE GENERATOR PLANT

If the welder has his torch lit and can conveniently leave his work for a few minutes to weld a job of comparative insignificance, a charge of 50c might be both just and profitable, but if the weld is to be made on the knotter of a binder, the charge could justly be proportionately higher. For instance if the selling price of the piece is $5.00 and the express charges 40c, the actual cost of a new piece would be $5.40. The time required to get this piece from the dealer, might be two days, during, which time the binder would be out of commission. If in welding the old piece, the welder uses 75c worth of gas and one hour's time at 35c it would actually cost him $1.10 to do the work but in this instance he would be amply justified in a charge of $4.00.

To determine the actual cost of work one would proceed as follows. Two drums, one hundred feet each at 2c per foot, would cost $8.00, to this would be added freight and cartage, which might come to $1.00, making a total cost of $9.00 for 400 feet or 2¼ cents per foot. The acetylene, if purchased in drums, would be calculated the same way; but if it is generated in the shop, one would consider the cost of carbide. One hundred pounds of carbide at 3¾c comes to $3.75 plus 40c for freight and cartage makes a total of $4.15 per hundred pounds carbide. This will generate 450 feet of acetylene which puts the cost of acetylene at about 9-10 of a cent per foot.

From the table, in the back of this book, may be learned the amount of each gas the various sized tips, used during one hour of continuous burning. To find the cost of gas, used on a job, would simply require multiplying the quantity used per hour by the number of hours in use, and that, by the cost per foot.

To do a certain job of welding, we will suppose it required 3 hours time, 90 feet of oxygen, 87 feet of acetylene, 10 pounds of charcoal, and one pound of welding rod, and it is desired to figure the cost. A typical procedure would be as follows:

```
   3 hours time, at 35c ................$ 1.05
  90 ft oxygen, at 2¼c ...              2.02
  87 ft. acetylene, at 1c ...            .87
                                       ------
                                       $ 3.94
Double for over head charges...........     2
                                       ------
                                       $ 7.88
 1 lb. welding rod, at 10c.               .10
10 lbs. charcoal, at 1c.                  .10
                                       ------
     Total cost ..                     $ 8.08
     50% profit on work                  4.04
                                       ------
     Charges for work..                $12.12
```

The purposes for doubling the cost of labor and gases for

overhead charges, is to cover the cost of maintaining and operating the shop, including rent, heat, light, insurance, bad accounts, etc.

```
          OXYGEN ACETYLENE WELDING CO.
                   TIME CARD
                              Job. No.
         Date                 Tag No
         Workman              Tag No..
                              Tag No.
                              Tag No..
Hrs. Labor
Hrs Overtime
Tip No.            ...Hrs.
Tip No.            . .Hrs..
Hrs. Oil Torch
Lbs. Charcoal
Lbs. Asbestos
Lbs. Asbestos Cement
Lbs. Cast Iron
Lbs. Steel
Lbs. Aluminum
Lbs. Bronze
Lbs. Copper
Misc. Material


Description of work
```

Fig 29

CONVENIENT TIME CARD FOR WELDING SHOPS

CHAPTER X.
WELDING RODS AND FLUXES.

The Theory of Fluxes:—Fluxes are used to clean the surfaces of the metals, to remove or prevent the accumulation of impurities by uniting with them before they combine with the metals, and sometimes, to lower the melting temperature The action is purely a chemical one and the task of preparing or preparing or prescribing suitable fluxes for the various metals, should only be undertaken by one who is thoroughly familiar with their chemical reactions.

The physical and chemical properties of the various metals are so different that a flux which would be suitable for welding one material would be ruinous to another. To illustrate, phosphorus contained in copper alloys, increases their strength and toughness; but one tenth of one per cent in steel causes it to be very brittle. Phosphorus has a great affinity for oxygen and when incorporated in melted copper, it will unite with the oxygen which the copper absorbs, and burn out taking the oxygen with it, but with iron, for which phosphorus has a greater affinity, this is different, when phosphorus is incorporated in melted iron it does not combine with oxygen, but remains in the iron and makes it brittle.

The Theoretical flux for each of the metals would be a substance that would combine with the gaseous impurities which are brought in contact with the melted metal, and after combining, will be liberated and pass off as a gas, or form a slag that will float on the surface. Since the service of a flux is in chemically uniting with objectionable impurities and removing them, and since this chemical union can only occur in a definite proportion, it follows, that if more flux is used than will chemically unite with the element to be removed, it will be free to unite with something else and become a new objection For this reason fluxes should be used strictly in accordance with the instructions given by the manufacturers.

The gaseous impurity, usually combated by fluxes is oxygen, but in some metals, such as, copper, bronze, and aluminum, there are other gases that may be absorbed unless their absorbtion is prevented by the presence of a suitable flux. In instances of this kind the formula for the fluxes, are sometimes quite complicated and to avoid the excessive use of certain chemicals they are frequently incorporated in the welding rod. Then by using these rods with the fluxes designed for them, the gases are completely absorbed and eliminated.

To weld *wrought iron, steel castings, steel plates and forgings*, no flux should be required; but a special steel welding rod is furnished in which the metaloids are combined in the right proportion to give the best results

Cast Iron requires a flux to destroy the oxide, which is less fusible than the metal, and which interposes itself in the welds and prevents the perfect joining of the molten metal. The action of the flux is to lower the melting temperature of the iron oxide, which will then float to the surface where it may be removed.

The welding rods should be selected according to their silicon content. The right proportions of silicon tend to eliminate the oxide from the iron.

Coppers—When copper and the copper alloys are melted they absorb oxygen, hydrogen, and carbon dioxide gases and to combat these gases is a problem that has not been solved until recently. The first attempts to absorb these gases into flux resulted in changing the texture of the weld; but today the manufacturers are supplying a flux to be used with a special welding rod, and the results obtained with them are eminently satisfactory.

It follows from what we have just explained, that the manufacture of welding materials containing deoxidizing elements, is extremely delicate, and necessitates rigorous supervision and control.

Welders who use the oxy-acetylene process in manufacturing and repairing, are by no means disposed to analyze or examine micrographically, the materials they are putting into their welds, and since these precautions are necessary to the production of reputable welding materials, it is well to shoulder the responsibility on a trustworthy manufacturer whose success depends on your success.

The selection of rods and fluxes for the different metals will be treated fully under the subject of welding.

CHAPTER XI.

GENERAL NOTES ON WELDING.

Time used in preparing for the weld is well spent. In a few days, a welder can acquire sufficient skill in handling the torch, to perform a fairly good weld, under favorable circumstances; but to do equally good work under any circumstance, requires thought, study and experience.

The primary object is to secure a weld that will be homogenous in texture, free from blow-holes, hard spots or scale, void of internal strains, and to leave the piece free from distortion The first three features mentioned are obtained in the actual performance of welding, and will be treated fully in a later paragraph, but to leave work, void of strains and distortion requires preparation in the way of preheating.

Cleaning:—It is unnecessary to spend much time in cleaning, scraping, or brightening the part to be welded, as would be required for brazing or soldering. The only requisite in this line is to remove the mud or grease by wiping. Other impurities burn or are melted and float to the surface where they may be scraped off with a rod.

Beveling:—If the piece to be welded is thicker than ⅛ of an inch, some time and advantage may be gained by beveling the edges, to enable the flame to enter between them, and the weld started at the bottom and built up. In pieces thinner than ⅛ of an inch, it is only necessary to separate the edges about 1-16 of an inch, to obtain the same advantage. If the pieces are very thin, like sheet iron of 14 gauge and lighter, they are liable to give some trouble by warping and buckling, and as the welding continues there may be a tendency for them to overlap each other. If this overlapping is permitted it will not only make the operation of welding more difficult, but it will destroy the intended shape of the article being welded. The operator should, therefore, carefully watch that the edges do not overlap, and if they can be bent up at right angles to a height of 1-16 of an inch it will make the work much easier. The bent up edges are melted and furnish welding material.

The amount of advantage gained in beveling, depends on the thickness of the piece, and the method of beveling. The object being to enable the operator to melt the material in the bottom and sides of the fracture and fill the gap with new material melted from the end of the welding rod. To secure a thorough and strong job, it is easily understood that this process must include the whole fractured surface, otherwise there will be a portion unwelded, and unless the edges are cut away or beveled, it will be necessary to melt the material and blow or scrape it out, to be certain that the welding includes the entire fractured surface Fig 34 and 35 show the method of beveling pieces ⅛ inch to ¼ inch thick.

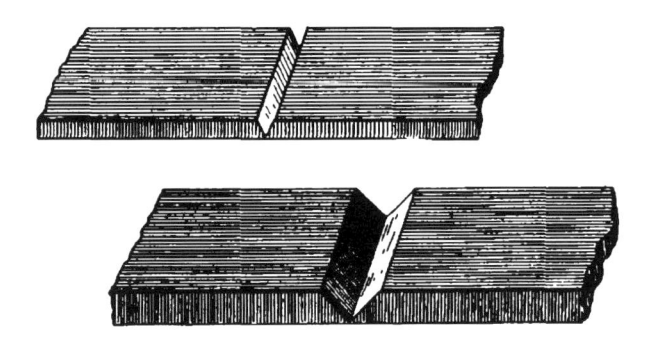

Figures 34 and 35
PRACTICAL METHOD OF BEVELING THIN PIECES

In work of this kind it is practical to bevel one side only; but in thicker material, if access can be had to the reverse side, a saving may be obtained by beveling both sides as shown in Fig 36.

This can not always be done, for the reverse side may not be accessible; but the work and expense is reduced about one-half and there is greater assurance of a thorough weld, when the work is done from both sides. The beginner is very liable to sacrifice good work for neatness and appearance It is much easier to do a neat looking job by simply welding on the surface; but this practice is positively to be condemned, and although a deep weld may look scattered and irregular the beginner should train himself until deep welding becomes instinctive or habitual.

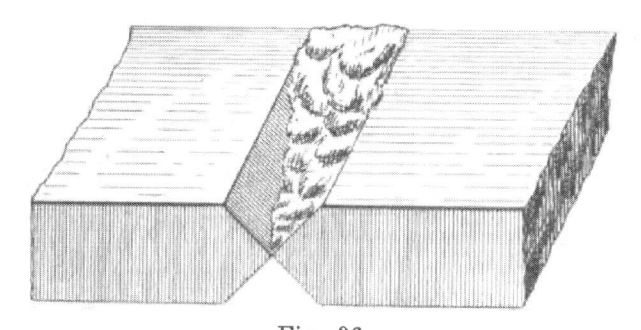

Fig. 36

METHOD OF BEVELING THICK PIECES

A weld which is made from both sides will look neater because the breadth of the fused surface will be narrower, and it can be more quickly finished, because the area of the cross section through the weld is only half as great, consequently there is only half as much metal to melt and fill in. This is more clearly illustrated in Figs. 37 and 38.

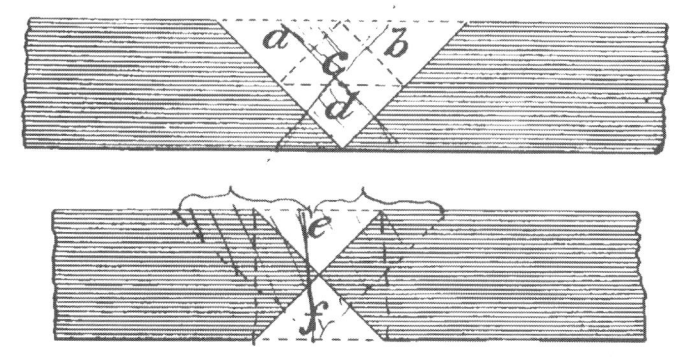

Figures 37 and 38

ILLUSTRATING THE ECONOMY OF BEVELING ON BOTH SIDES

in which the area is divided into triangles having equal area. This illustration is self explanatory, it being necessary to merely count the nnmber of triangles in each figure, to ascertain the comparative areas.

Precautions Regarding Expansion:—The phenomenon of expansion is explained on page 32 under the chapter on physics, and it is here proposed to explain to the welder, how this phenomenon may effect his success or defeat according to his understanding, and preparation to provide for it.

When metal is heated it will expand and there is no evading it. Sometimes trouble occurs when expansion is taking place. At other times it does not develop until after the metal commences to shrink, or resume its original proportions. The result of expansion and contraction often produces the most unexpected effects, and the welder is admonished to give this subject much earnest thought. No text book can tell him what may happen or what to do on every occasion that may develop during his welding career; these are things that must be studied out by himself, and his ultimate success depends as much on his ability to overcome the effects of expansion as on his ability to handle the torch. So do not pass this subject until you are thoroughly determined to observe, study and solve the capers that expansion will play with you during your earlier efforts. Sometimes the effect of expansion can be ignored, and the welder will soon learn by experience, when this will be true. A good illustration of this is in figures 39 and 40.

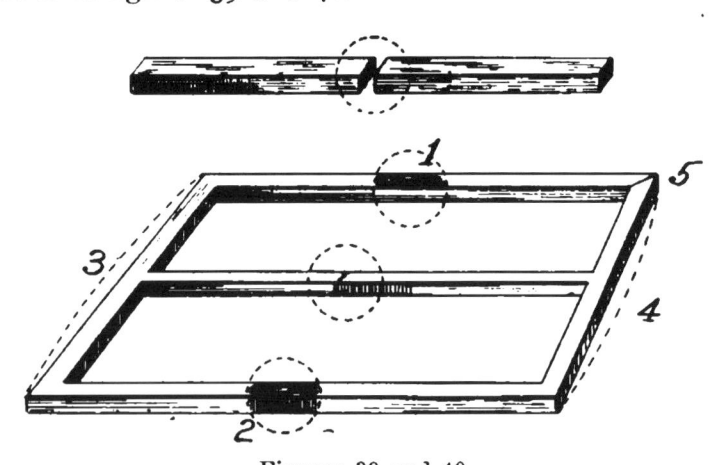

Figures 39 and 40

EFFECTS OF EXPANSION AND CONTRACTION

In Fig 39, no bad effects of expansion are to be feared because the ends are free to move and extend or withdraw. On the contrary in Fig 40 the same bar having the same break, is the center member in a two panel frame. What will be the effect of expansion in this case? As the metal in the vicinity of the weld becomes heated it will expand. The ends being a part of the frame at 3 and 4 will be held in their normal position; but the melted portion surrounding the weld will offer no resistance, and the expansion will push the melted ends closer together in the weld. When the job is finished, and the metal begins to cool off, shrinkage takes place and the center bar shortens. If the metal is elastic or ductile the shrinkage may not cause a break, but will cause a strain or deformation of the frame. This would probably be the case with mild steel; but with cast iron, it would likely cause a break in the hottest place, which would be in the newly welded portion. Neglect to provide for expansion would therefore cause failure.

Copper, aluminum, cast iron, and those metals that are weakest when hot, will usually break in the weld.

On reflection, it will be observed that, to make a success of this job, it is only necessary to preheat the portion of the frame, indicated at 1 and 2, then on cooling the shrinkage will be equal in each of the parallel bars, and no break or distortion will result.

If it is impossible to heat the frame, as described above, other methods are at the disposal of the welder; for example, a slight spreading of the two bars 3 and 4, to the position indicated by the dotted lines. This may be done with keys, wedges, or jackscrews, and the effect is to separate or spread the fracture. While making the weld, expansion takes place, as described before, but when the weld is finished and shrinkage commences the wedges or screws are removed, and as the center bar shortens, the sides gradually resume their former position, and the frame is void of strains or fracture.

Another method, which is not especially recommended except on rare occasions, is to cut the frame at 5, then weld the fracture and the cut will accommodate the expansion by spreading, then after the center bar has been welded and shrunken, the cut in the corner can be welded, where the effects of expansion and contraction need not be feared.

There has recently come into use, a method of restricting the expansion to a very limited portion, resulting in the expansion being so slight that it may be ignored. This is done by allowing the portion immediately surrounding the weld, to attain the required temperature; but preventing the heat spreading, which of course will reduce the expansion, by cooling the surrounding portion with water.

If restricting the amount and extent of expansion is all that is to be desired, this method might give satisfactory results; but there are other causes that may produce failure. One of these is chilling the metal. For reasons that will be explained later it is desirable to have the weld and surrounding metal as hot as it can be made without changing its shape, or texture, and if the cooling method is used to eliminate expansion, the heat of the portion being welded, will be conducted away, and it will be impossible to maintain a temperature that will give the best results.

The Economy of Preheating:—Preheating is essential as an economic measure. To properly execute a weld, the sides and bottom of the fracture must be melted, and if the metal is cold it will require more of the welder's time, and more gas to bring it up to the melting temperature, than if it had been previously heated with a cheaper fuel in a manner that did not require the constant attention of the operator. Therefore, to obtain the greatest measure of economy, the piece to be welded should be placed in a preheating furnace, and allowed to heat up while the welder is doing something else.

Preheating to Eliminate Defects in the Weld:—It has been explained under the chapter on metallurgy called "Metals and Their Properties," that, when melted cast iron or high carbon steel comes in contact with a cold metallic surface, it chills and becomes so hard that it cannot be machined or filed. It is not an uncommon thing to find hard spots in a cast iron weld, which have been caused in this way.

Cast iron contains more impurities than any of the ferrous group, and when it is melted, these impurities form a gas and, if the metal is sufficiently fluid, they will float to the surface in bubbles and be liberated; but if the melted metal is not perfectly fluid, these bubbles will remain in the bath and show blow holes in the weld.

In heavy sections of cast iron that have not been preheated, the melted metal is chilled so rapidly by the surrounding cold portion, that it cannot be kept sufficiently fluid for these gas bubbles to raise.

Considering the foregoing it may be said, that the practice of preheating cannot well be eliminated.

How and Where to Preheat:—An article like an automobile cylinder or motor frame should be heated throughout, so that the whole piece will be hot and expand in all directions alike. This is also true of any other small intricate piece that may become badly distorted or broken by unequal expansion; but in the case of a large flywheel or gear, with one or two broken spokes, it would be cumbersome, expensive and unnecessary to preheat the whole wheel.

Large articles of this nature are only preheated in a portion which must be selected according to the location of the break. This portion will usually include the hub and a little over one-half of the rim, including the broken portion. The preheating furnace for this kind of work will be a temporary affair built of loosely piled brick, with an asbestos covering One side is semi-circular, and follows the contour of the wheel, and the other side is straight, fitting around the spokes and rim. The arrangement of air drafts must accommodate the nature of the work

Adjusting the Flame:—One of the first things the welder will note, is the peculiar appearance of the flame issuing from the tip of his torch. When this is in normal working condition there will be an inner white flame of dazzling brightness, surrounded by an outer flame of a pale bluish tinge, with a wide yellow border. When this inner flame is at the maximum size attainable, and has a clear distinct outline, the flame is said to be neutral. That is, it will have neither an oxidizing or carbonizing effect on the weld. With very few exceptions, this is the kind of flame that should be obtained before starting to weld. Manipulating the valves to produce this kind of flame is called adjusting the torch. The method of procedure, to attain this adjustment, is described as follows:

After connecting the torch and regulators as described in chapter 8, the operator will see that all valves are open except those in the regulators, these will be closed by unscrewing the handle until it is quite free and does not bear on the springs within. Starting from this position the operator will screw in the handle on the *Acetylene* regulator until the gas begins to flow, and then ignite it. Continue to screw in the valve handle, until the base of the flame appears to leave the torch and stand away about an eighth of an inch.

The acetylene flame is now a large, flaring, smoky, irregular shaped mass; but screw in the handle on the *oxygen* regulator, and the flame will commence to assume definite size and proportion. Continue to slowly open this valve and there will appear an inner white flame that blends with a thin feathery edge into a pale blue outer flame.

As the oxygen supply is increased, this inner white flame becomes smaller and the outline more distinct and, when this thin feathery edge is entirely gone, the inner flame will be about three times longer than in diameter, and have a distinct outline. This is a neutral flame, and is the proper flame for welding.

Handling the Torch:—Having the edges of the metal beveled as described before, and placed parallel, the flame of the torch is directed into the V shaped groove formed by the bevel. The metal on the sides and bottom of the groove is melted until it is quite fluid, then the end of the welding rod is brought under the flame and when it commences to melt it is submerged in the metal melted from the sides of the groove.

The flame and welding rod are kept continually in motion, the rod following close behind the flame, repeatedly dodging in and out from under it with a little circular motion; but always submerged in the melted metal and always hot enough to be continuously melting and feeding the weld with new material.

The torch will be advanced along the line of the weld just as fast as the sides and bottom will melt, and become thoroughly fluid, while the frequency of the circular movements of the rod and the length of time it remains under the flame, will be timed to fill the weld as fast as the torch advances. The flame and rod should always be together.

At first the welder will be bothered by having his welding rod freeze to the weld, which will have to be melted loose again

GENERAL NOTES ON WELDING

with the torch; but he should be undaunted by these little events for they only serve to remind him that his welding rod must always be melting hot and submerged in melted metal.

It takes practice to acquire the knack of having the torch and rod continually in motion describing little circles, keeping them close together, regulating the melting rate of the rod to fill the weld as fast as the sides of the groove are melted and become fit to receive new material; but the knack is acquired with only a few days of persistent effort.

The melting of the welding rod and the edges of the weld must take place at the same time, and the rod stirred in the puddle of melted metal, to make the two metals alloy immediately with each other.

If the rod flows between the edges of the weld before they are melted, the weld will be bad.

The melting rod should never fall in drops on the weld.

Fig. 41
THE MELTING ROD SHOULD NOT DRIP INTO THE WELD.

The torch should be held so that the end of the white flame is ⅛ to ⅜ of an inch away from the work, the distance being proportional to the size of the tip and the nature of the work. For a medium sized tip a good average distance would be ¼ of an inch. Extreme care must be taken to not permit the end of the tip to touch the melted metal, or to allow the melted metal to splash into the tip.

Movements of the Torch:—An advantage may be gained by giving the torch a slight circular movement to direct the flame rotatively against one side of the weld, back onto the welding rod, over to the other side of the weld, then forward onto the unmelted portion and thus continue in a series of little circles, of uniform size and regular frequency. The diameter of the circles should be nearly equal to the breadth of the weld.

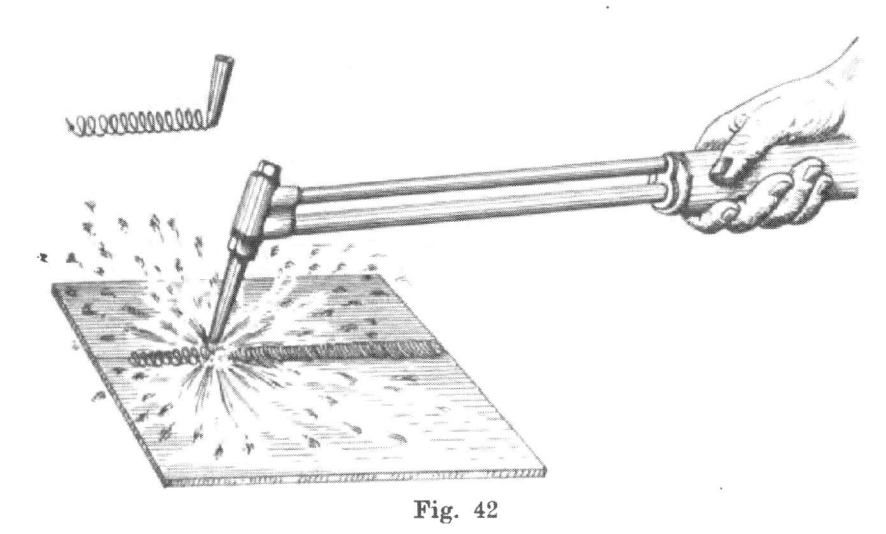

Fig. 42

CIRCULAR MOVEMENT OF TORCH FOR WORK OF MEDIUM THICKNESS

For welds of greater thickness a side to side movement may give better results. The amount of the movement corresponding with the breadth of the weld, and regulated in time to the melting of the sides. These movements are however only suggestions, and the welder must decide for himself what course he will pursue.

Fig. 43

SIDE TO SIDE MOVEMENT OF THE TORCH FOR HEAVIER WELDS

There are certainly manipulations to be learned, but they are relatively easy to acquire, and are better obtained by practice than by reading.

The beginner usually does not melt enough and the weld lacks penetration, or he melts too much, and so makes holes. It is evidently necessary to find a happy medium, and above all to work regularly.

Filling in Holes:—Holes are particularly despairing to the beginner, because in trying to mend them, he usually sees them enlarge. A few instructions on filling these holes will be appropriate here. The flame should be inclined until it is almost parallel with the surface of the work and directed against the edge of the material. As soon as the metal begins to get plastic, a little metal is welded to the edge, from the welding rod. Continue this process until the hole is filled. The principal difficulty encountered in this work is to regulate the heat so that it will not melt the edges away or cause the welding rod to drip through the opening.

Fig. 44
POSITION OF TORCH FOR FILLING HOLES

Defects of Welds:—During the process of welding there are several defects that may develop and to avoid them the welder is admonished to be constantly alert to the causes that may produce them.

The first, is lack of penetration. This more frequently takes place when the edges of the weld are not beveled; the heat has not been sufficient to melt through the metal, and the original crack shows on the reverse side. This not only effects the solidity of the weld, but affords a starting point for a new break.

To avoid this defect, one must not go to the other extreme and melt holes through the piece, for these holes cause loss of heat and time, and assist oxidation.

Next there is adhesion. This very significant term is difficult to explain. One obtains adhesion in different ways, either by not sufficiently melting the edge of the weld, or by doing so unequally. It may also be done by flowing melted metal onto parts that have not been previously melted, or have cooled off, and again by interposition of oxide in the bath.

Welders should exercise constant care to avoid "adhesion" for it is not rare to find this defect in welds made by experienced workmen. Melted metal flowing from the edges of the weld into the bottom, will cause the same defect, if the bottom is not melted.

There are sometimes bad joints due to the interposition of a layer of oxide between the old and new metal, this is generally due to piling melted metal on metal that has solidified, or to lack of liquefaction in the molten bath.

Blow holes frequently form in the weld and the strength of the joint suffers accordingly. These blow holes may be due to lack of preheating, to absorption of gases, or to blowing air into the melted metal with the torch The elimination of the first two defects will be treated under the subject of welding the different metals.

We must mention lastly that welds are sometimes insufficiently filled The level of the weld does not reach the surface of the piece. Such defects are attributed entirely to carelessness.

Welding Wrought Iron and Mild Steel:—Wrought iron and mild steel are the easiest metals to weld by the autogenous process. They require no flux to absorb oxides or other impurities.

A steel welding rod is used and by following the instructions given in the preceding paragraphs of this chapter, the welder is provided with all the instructions he may require. The only other thing needed is practice.

Welding Cast Iron:—When everything is taken into consideration, the difficulties to be overcome in welding cast iron, are neither numerous or insurmountable, as a matter of fact when cast iron is properly welded the joint is stronger than the original piece This is generally due to the superior quality of the iron put into the weld.

In the chapter on metals and their properties, we learned that cast iron contained a large amount of carbon That this carbon existed in the cast iron in two conditions, that is, the combined condition as white iron and in the free or graphite condition as gray iron. We also learned that the gray iron was soft and that the white iron was very hard, and could not be machined.

Since the majority of welds in cast iron should be capable of being machined, it is indispensable that the weld should be in the condition of gray iron.

When welding rods of proper consistency are used, a good soft gray iron weld can be obtained by protecting it against chilling while the melted metal is being run in. This may be done by preheating and pursuing the methods prescribed to prevent adhesion.

Cast iron requires a flux to destroy the iron oxide, which is less fusible than the metal and which interposes itself in the weld and prevents the perfect joining of the molten metal. The action of the flux is to lower the melting temperature of the oxide, which will then float to the surface where it may be removed. The flux is used by putting the end of the hot welding rod into the box of flux and then working it into the weld.

Cast iron is laden with impurities which form gases when the iron is melted. If the melted iron is kept sufficiently fluid these gases will come to the surface and disappear, but if the metal is in only a semi-fluid state they will remain in the bath and cause a spongy weld. This trouble is more noticeable in heavy work, which, if not preheated, will chill the melted metal so quickly that the gases cannot escape.

The elimination of these gases may be assisted by rotating the torch around in a little pool and then gradually withdrawing it; but in so doing the welder should be careful to not blow air and gases into the melted metal. Thoroughly preheating the casting will also greatly assist in eliminating the blow holes.

Welding Malleable Cast Iron:—While the process of autogenous welding is being used so successfully in all the metal trades, many unsuccessful attempts have been made to weld malleable cast iron, and to those who have experienced disappointment, an explanation of why their efforts failed, with an outline of a method by which these castings can be mended, should be of benefit.

Malleable castings are first made in the condition of hard brittle, white cast iron and subsequently made malleable by heat treatment. The heating process which converts white cast iron to malleable iron is called annealing, and effects a chemical change in the structure by decarbonization. This decarbonization is nearly complete at the surface and penetrates in a lessening degree toward the center, giving the outside portion the texture of mild steel while the inner portion may retain, in a more or less degree, the qualities of cast iron. When this metal is remelted the carbon is dispersed, and the entire mass reverts to cast iron.

The operator who is used to welding mild steel and cast iron will recall that they are handled differently. That the method used in welding steel to steel would be useless in welding cast iron, or the methods employed with cast iron would be equally unsuccessful with steel. That is practically what he is trying to do when he undertakes to weld a malleable casting. The material is not homogenous. The bottom portion of the weld being in cast iron, and the top portion in steel, with no definite dividing line between, it is useless to follow the method prescribed for either, and to his trouble is added the difficulty occasioned by the diffusion of the elements in the material melted from the sides of the fracture.

It follows that to successfully mend a malleable casting the process employed must not necessitate melting the sides of the fracture, that the welding material should fuse at a lower temperature than the casting, and that its adherence, bonding qualities, physical strength and ductility should closely resemble the original casting. After much study and experiment, the Vulcan Process Company and their allied interests in Minneapolis are having considerable success in mending broken malleable castings, and a description of their methods will undoubtedly be useful to others who are employed in the metal trades.

In preparing the work for mending, the fracture is chipped away in the form of a V groove with the pointed bottom just coming to the surface on the opposite side, or, if the casting is thick and the opposite side accessible, two grooves are cut with their pointed bottoms meeting in the center. The part surrounding the fracture is then heated with an oxy-acetylene torch to a bright red, and sprinkled with Vulcan bronze flux followed by a few drops of Tobin bronze melted from the welding rod. If the bronze remains in a little globule the work is not hot enough, but if it spreads and adheres to the surface, the temperature is right, and the groove should be quickly filled It is not advisable to keep the work hot any longer than is necessary, but to make the mend as quickly and at as low a temperature as possible. The behavior of the bronze affords a guide in regulating the temperature.

This process cannot be called autogenous welding, but a malleable casting mended in this way is practically as good as one piece. It has about the same tensile strength and ductility as the original and the process has the advantage of being very quickly performed.

Welding Copper, Brass and Bronze:—Copper and all of its alloys have a faculty of absorbing gases from the flame. The oxide of copper is very soluble in the metal and forms, with it, an alloy which crystallizes in the mass and destroys the homogeneous texture of the weld.

If the autogenous welding of copper is obtained by melting the edges and adding metal melted from a pure copper welding rod, there will necessarily be considerable oxidation of the metal and the oxide will remain in the weld. The metal will lose its distinctive properties and be riddled with blow holes. No manipulation or regulation of the torch can overcome these defects

It is therefore necessary to use a deoxidizer capable of reducing the oxide as it is formed. Since the oxide is dissolved in the metals itself, the use of a flux does not give the expected results. It is therefore necessary that the deoxidizer be incorporated in the welding rod, so that it will be diffused continuously throughout the molten metal. All welds made on red copper, without the use of deoxidizing welding rods, are therefore strongly oxidized and full of blow holes.

The tensile strength of copper diminishes rapidly as the temperature is raised and unless the welder uses precautions to relieve the weld of strains while it is hot, it will be very likely to crack. These strains may be relieved by heating other parts of the piece.

The weld should be prepared exactly the same as for welding iron or steel, and the torch manipulated the same as described before

On account of the conductivity of this metal, it might be advisable to use a larger tip, on the torch, than would be used for welding steel The flame of the torch should be perfectly regulated and maintained without excess of either gas, for if either acetylene or oxygen is free in the flame it will be absorbed in the weld

Brasses and bronzes require the same precautions and welding rods as are used for copper; but on account of their containing other metals, it is necessary to use a bronze flux in addition to deoxidizing welding rods.

Welding Aluminum.—When aluminum is melted it oxidizes very freely and this oxide which clings to the surface of the metal, prevents the joining of the new metal to the old It is therefore necessary to remove this oxide, which is done by scraping it out after the metal is melted. Aluminum melts at a comparatively low temperature and, since the welder is not warned of the approaching melting temperature, by any change in color, he must use care not to melt the whole structure and destroy it. This may occur in the preheating fire unless caution is used. Aluminum like copper is very weak when hot and this property combined with the excessive expansion of the metal, is something that may cause the weld to break soon after its completion unless precautions are taken to remove shrinkage strains, by preheating.

Some writers advocate the use of a deoxidizing flux for making aluminum welds; but others believe better welds may be obtained by the "puddle" system of welding than by the use of fluxes. It is the writer's observation, that excellent welds are being made today by the puddle system, and since this method is very easily learned, it will be described here.

The Puddle System.—Aside from the oxy-acetylene torch and welding rods of the purest aluminum, the only tool used is a long slender steel rod, flattened on the end to form a paddle or spoon This rod is called a spatula Armed with this tool the welder will melt the metal where the weld is to be made and with the spatula, scrape off the surface, leaving it clean and bright This only removes the dirt for, although it may not be visible, oxide forms on the bright surface immediately behind the spatula, and unless it is broken up the new metal will not join. Breaking up this oxide is done after the surface is covered with new melted metal, which protects it from further oxidation and is accomplished by gently scraping the spatula through the mass of melted aluminum and removing it.

The operation is somewhat similar to scraping the skin off melted babbit; the only difference being, that the oxide of aluminum may be mixed with the melted metal. The success of the weld depends on the thoroughness of this skinning or puddling operation.

After a little metal is added and thoroughly puddled, more aluminum is melted in and the puddling repeated.

The precautions to be taken in welding aluminum are similar to those described before. It is of primary importance to never add new metal to a surface that is not in a molten condition.

Lead Burning:—The process called burning is used for joining the edges of lead sheets or pipes without solder. The edges are fused to an extent which permits the parts to unite and form one solid piece when cooled. This process is known as the autogenous process, and although it has been practised for centuries, it is used far less at the present day than it should be. It affords a quick and cheap method of making lead joints of the most durable character, and it may be used with profit in many cases instead of the soldering process now commonly employed.

Solder cannot be used for joints which are exposed to contact with acids, because most of the ordinary acids will dissolve the tin, of which the solder is in part composed.

Tanks which are used for the manufacture or storage of acids or acid salts, or for the storage of mineral oils, petroleum, etc, are usually lined with lead. The joints in these linings, and in all of the lead pipes which are used for the same purpose, must be made by burning.

The operation is performed by melting the edges to be joined a drop at a time, by means of a torch. It is essential that the flame which is used shall not oxidize or tarnish the metal. If the drop of melted metal does oxidize, it will not unite with the solid parts, and the joint will be a failure.

The most certain and convenient way to secure a non-oxidizing flame is to use hydrogen gas mixed with air to supply the torch. Other methods may be employed, but none are so convenient as the hydrogen gas process.

A FEW EXAMPLES IN WELDING.

In describing a few examples on welding, we will consider that the welder has acquired a knowledge in handling his torch and welding the various kind of materials, so this detail will be omitted, and the illustration confined to a description of the preparation incidental to the particular example.

Welding a Crank Shaft:—The difficulties is welding a crank shaft as shown in Figure 45, are not in the performance of welding; but in providing for expansion and securing alignment, that will obviate the necessity of much machine work.

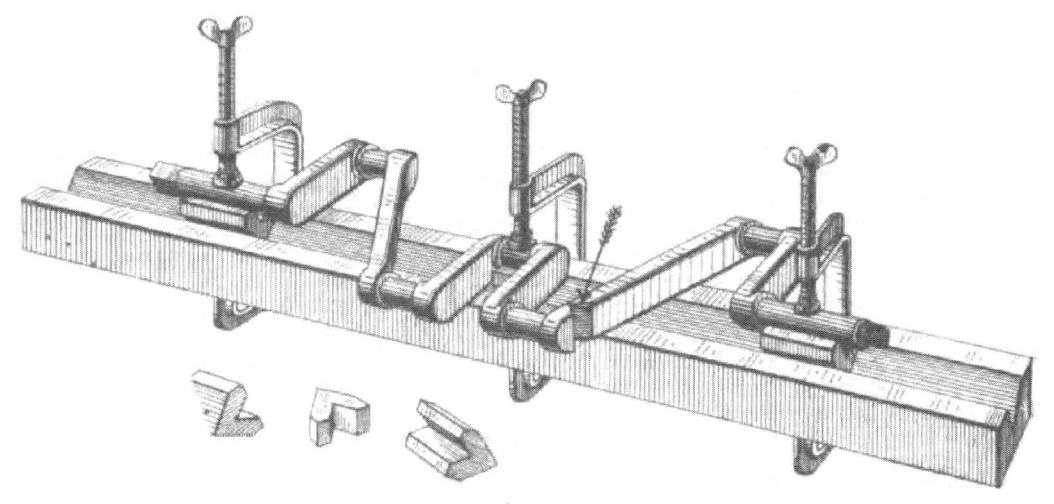

Fig. 45

CRANK SHAFT ON V BLOCKS PREPARED FOR WELDING

Before assembling for welding the fracture is ground away to form a V groove, as is usual in preparing any weld, but in this case there is about an eight of an inch of the fracture left undisturbed. This is to furnish a guide for adjusting the pieces. The shaft is then clamped in V blocks like those shown in the picture. These V blocks have a piece of cardboard or sheet iron placed between the sloping side of the block and the long V bar which holds them. In the picture above these pieces of sheet iron would be on the far side of the two blocks shown to the left and on the near side of the block shown to the right and when the crank shaft is clamped in position, they would cause an opening to show between the fractured ends of the crank shaft. This opening is to take care of expansion and should be about 1-32 of an inch. With the torch, the part surrounding the weld will be heated until this space is closed up by expansion, and then the V shaped opening welded full. Before shrinkage takes place the clamps and strips of sheet metal are removed, when this part of the weld become rigid, the unwelded portion on the back is melted out and welded full.

Welding the Inner Wall of an Auto Cylinder:—A portion of the water jacket, outside the fracture, is cut out by drilling as shown in Figure 46.

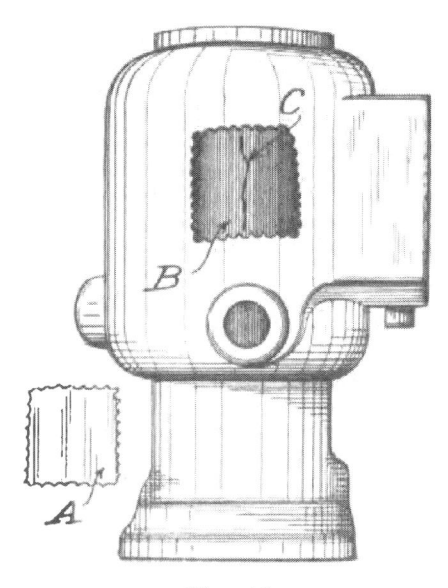

Fig. 46
AUTO CYLINDER PREPARED FOR WELDING

The whole cylinder is then put into a preheating fire with the fractured side up and when sufficiently heated the covering is layed aside and the fracture melted away with the torch and

GENERAL NOTES ON WELDING

welded full. The piece which was cut out of the water jacket is then welded back into place. For convenience in holding this piece in place while it is being fastened, a small rod may be welded in the center, to form a handle.

WELDING AUTO SPRINGS.

The usual method in welding auto springs, is to first bring the spring to its normal position and block it up with bricks to hold it in alignment while it is being welded. Then with the oxy-acetylene torch the fracture is quickly melted and run together

The process differs from welding mild steel in the fact that the edges of mild steel plates are separated a short distance to facilitate the flame entering between them, the space being filled with material melted from the welding rod, but when welding springs, the edges are brought tight together and a narrow strip of the material adjoining the fracture is melted from the top down through to the bottom, adding only as much material from the welding rod as is required to restore the normal thickness. When this has been done on one side it is repeated on the other; but this time it is not necessary to weld as deep.

The portion of the spring, which has just been welded, is a little softer than the rest and is not as liable to break from shock It is not the custom to retemper this part of the spring for very good results are obtained without. To make this part of the same temper as the rest, would require retempering the whole spring, which is an undertaking not to be recommended to any one who is not skilled in that line and provided with a suitable heating furnace and oil bath. Even then it is a treacherous job and better results are usually obtained by leaving the weld un tempered

It is well for the reader to refer to the illustrations on page 1, 2, and 7 and note the temporary grates which were constructed to sustain the preheating fire.

CHAPTER XII.

CUTTING IRON AND STEEL WITH THE OXYGEN JET.

The rapid combustion of iron in oxygen has been known for over a century and was mentioned by Lavoisier. The chemical treatise on this subject mention that iron oxide formed is more fusible than the iron and is detached as the combustion proceeds, continually exposing the bare iron to the attack of the oxygen.

It is this phenomenon that makes possible the rapid cutting of iron and steel, with a torch and oxygen jet, and although it has been known so long it was not until recent years that the process was used industrially.

All thicknesses can be cut from the thinnest sheets to heavy armor plates for battle ships. The process is also being used extensively in steel foundries for cutting the gates and risers from steel castings. In fact the uses to which it may be advantageously applied are innumerable, and as people become better acquainted with it, they are finding new uses for it. On pages 5 and 6 are mentioned a few of the recent applications of this process, to cutting the wreckage of ore-docks and sunken ships.

The Theory:—All instructions in autogenous welding caution the operator to use a perfectly neutral flame, for if he uses too much oxygen, he is told, the metal will become oxidized, or burned up. If a small piece of iron, or steel is heated and dropped into oxygen it will burn rapidly. The iron actually becomes a fuel and is burned in the oxygen; and in burning it generates heat just the same as any other fuel would do in burning. This phenomenon which is so carefully avoided when making welds, is used to advantage in oxy-acetylene cutting. The torch is arranged to first deliver a hot neutral oxy-acetylene flame until the metal is at a white heat, then a jet of oxygen is impinged against this hot metal and iron burning or oxidation ensues.

The oxidation commences at the part which has previously been heated to redness, because at this temperature the reaction takes place more radiply. The combustion or burning of this portion of the iron, liberates heat, a portion of which is absorbed by the surrounding iron, and raises it to a red heat, so that in turn it burns. This burning is progressively extended by moving the torch along the line of the cut.

This burned iron is known to chemists as oxide of iron and when first formed it may appear as a solid scale adhering to the surface of the iron. If it remain there it protects the iron against any further oxidation or burning just the same as a thick covering of ashes will stop the burning of wood. Wrought iron and mild steel, melts at a much higher temperature than does the oxide of iron. So on these substances the oxide will melt first and run off leaving the surface of the metal clean, and continually exposed to the attacks of the oxygen jet.

The oxide on cast iron cannot be melted off to expose the clean surface to the attack of the oxygen jet, because its melting temperature is higher than that of the metal. It may be melted, but the metal melts first and the oxide mixes with it. The process is not the clean rapid cutting action obtained with mild steel, or wrought iron, but is merely one of melting. It is therefore said that cast iron cannot be cut by the oxy-acetylene process. This is also true of copper, brass, bronzes, aluminum, and very high carbon steel.

Using the Torch:—In using the oxy-acetylene cutting torch it is advisable to first adjust the regulator on the oxygen drum to deliver oxygen at 10 to 50 pounds pressure, according to thickness of the metal. Then turn on a little acetylene, ignite it, and open the needle valve in the handle of the torch until the base of the flame appears to leave the torch and stands away about an eighth of an inch. The acetylene flame is now a large, flaring, smoky, irregular shaped mass, but open the little needle valve that controls the oxygen supply and the flame will commence to assume definite size and proportion. Continue to slowly open this valve and there will appear an inner white flame that blends with a thin feathery edge into a pale blue outer flame, and as the oxygen supply is slowly increased this inner white flame becomes smaller, and the outline more distinct. When the thin feathery outline of this inner flame is entirely gone and the dividing line between the two parts of the flame is distinct, the oxygen supply is sufficient, and the flame is neutral.

To start the cutting action, the little white inner flame should be held about three sixteenths of an inch from the metal until it begins to melt, then the thumb lever is pressed which starts a flow of oxygen through the cutting tip. When the oxygen comes in contact with the metal it burns it very rapidly, and oxide of iron runs or is blown out of the cut. When starting a cut in the middle of a plate of steel, there is no place for this melted iron oxide to run out, so it gathers in a little puddle where the force of the torch blows and spatters it. In this event care should be taken to prevent it splashing into the end of the torch. This may be prevented by holding the torch a little farther away from the plate than would be necessary in starting the cut at the edge.

After the cut is started and there is a place for the iron oxide to escape, the torch may be brought a little closer to the work and steadily advanced without wabbling or tilting, moving evenly along the line of cut as fast as the metal will burn and run out. If the torch is held too far away, the action is slower and the gap of the cut is wider, while if it is too close, particles of burned iron may enter the torch. A jerky, wabbly movement makes a ragged cut. Plates, ⅛ or 3-16 inches thick, can be cut with the ordinary welding torch, by first heating the metal to a white heat with the oxy-acetylene flame and then shutting the acetylene entirely off and using the oxygen jet the same as in the regular cutting torch The heat of the burning steel is sufficient to cause the combustion of the adjoining material and thus the operation is continuous without the use of the preheating flame which accompanies the cutting torch.

The jerky wabbly movement, previously mentioned, not only makes a ragged cut, but it retards the progress of the cut and adds to the cost of the operation. In consequence of this, there have been cutting machines designed, which carry the torch at any desired angle and at a uniform speed across the work. To obtain the best results some arrangement of this kind is required.

In figure No. 47 is shown a machine of the kind just described, which is designed to cut bars or structural shapes. The piece to be cut is clamped in the V shaped notch, and the cutting torch,

CUTTING IRON AND STEEL WITH THE OXYGEN JET   113

which is easily discernable in the picture, is carried steadily across the work by means of a screw.

A simple device for cutting elliptical man holes in boiler plates, may be made by providing a track, of angle iron, formed to the shape of the desired manhole and equipped with a carriage to carry the torch. The carriage can be of the easiest construction, and provided with three wheels, two of which will ride on the track and one on the plate.

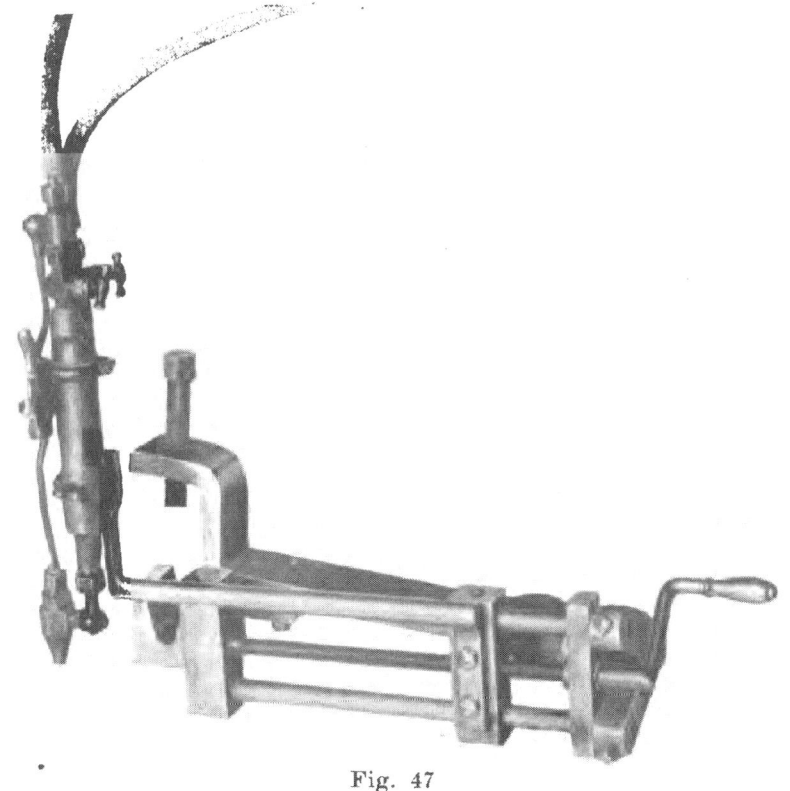

Fig. 47

MACHINE FOR CUTTING BARS AND STRUCTURAL SHAPES

The machine shown in the following figure No. 48 is designed for cutting circular plates or holes. The heavy base which serves as a center, is held in place by its weight, and affording a bearing for the upright stud which carries the horizontal bar. The bar slides through the stud and may be clamped in any position that will give the required diameter to the circle. After this adjustment has been made, the stud is rotated in the base, by hand, carrying the torch around in the path of a circle. The torch shown in these two illustrations is especially designed for machine use.

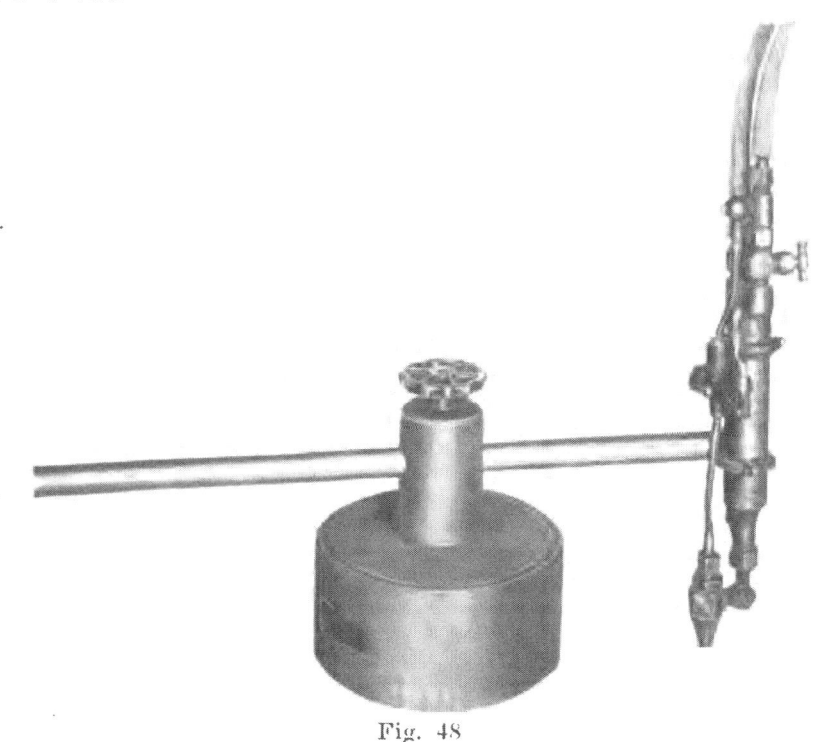

Fig. 48
MACHINE FOR CUTTING CIRCULAR PLATES AND OPENINGS

Structural iron workers, erecting contractors, and others engaged in building or tearing down old structures, find the oxygen cutting process of great service to them. The saving which results from its use may be judged by the reader, after noting the table of cutting speeds and costs as noted below.

Thickness of plate	Cost of gas @ 2c per foot		Time per foot in seconds
	Oxygen	Acetylene	
¼	$0.0082	$0.0026	24
½	0.0154	0.0034	30
1	0.0244	0.0042	38
1½	0.0306	0.0066	46

Fig. 49

CUTTING OLD STEEL FLOOR BEAMS

During the year 1914 the old union depot in Minneapolis was torn down to make room for a new building.

All the structural steel members in this building were removed by cutting them free, with the oxy-acetylene cutting torch. The above picture was made from a photo. of the cutters, while at work. The process was eminently successful and showed a great saving over the old method of removing them by knocking off the rivet heads, or sawing.

Fig. 50

REDUCING AN OLD BOILER TO SCRAP

It was recently required to remove an old steam boiler from the sub-basement of a department store. The boiler had been in use many years, during which time the building had been remodeled and brick walls built, in a way that required their destruction to remove the boiler in one piece. With the oxy-acetylene cutting torch the boiler was quickly reduced to scrap and removed in pieces.

Fig. 51
REDUCING AN OLD BOILER TO SCRAP

CHAPTER XIII.

BOILER MAKING AND SHEET METAL WORK.

There is perhaps no class of work where the oxy-acetylene cutting and welding processes can be used to better or as good advantage as in boiler and sheet metal work.

Boiler makers who consented to give the process a trial in their shops, were surprised and marveled at the savings they could realize by its continual use. Even then they had not learned of all the applications, of which this apparatus was capable, and every day they are finding new places where the process can save them time and money.

A Superintendent, of Motive Power, on one of our prominent railroads, recently made the statement that the oxy-acetylene plant in his shops, was saving for his company, an average of four dollars an hour, for every hour a torch is in use. The torch has such universal application, and the operations to which it can be advantageously applied, are so general and frequent, they can hardly be enumerated, but as the welder becomes familiar with the process he finds them himself.

To sustain these statements, we will cite a few instances where the operation proved its superiority over old methods.

Cutting a full door patch for a locomotive boiler, usually required 6 hours time for a boiler maker, and his helper, at an average total cost of $4.04. The same job done by the oxy-acetylene process, required nine minutes time and cost 25 cents for labor and gas.

Cutting a side sheet and door sheet by the old method, required 18 hours time of two men and usually cost $12.15. By the new method, the same work was done in thirty minutes at a cost of 83 cents.

Another incident is in welding an outside sheet. On previous occasions it required the work of two men for 16 hours and cost $10.80 to make the repair, which was welded with an oxy-acetylene torch in 3 hours time at a total cost of $5.85.

A cracked sheet, usually required patching and to do this at an average cost of $15.00 was good work, but with the oxy-acetylene process, the crack can be welded and the sheet made as good as new, at a cost of $4.00. The welded crack has an advantage over the patch, in the fact that it only presents one thickness of metal, to the action of the fire. This advantage is well appreciated by boiler makers.

To reduce an old boiler to commercial scrap, required the labor of two men for 80 hours and usually cost about $40.00 The same work can be done with one man using the oxy-acetylene torch in 7½ hours and will cost, for labor and gas, about $12.00

The question will probably occur to some practical boiler makers, whether an oxy-acetylene welded seam will withstand the action of fire. In answer to this we will cite an incident, in Duluth, where it was desired to construct a bosh jacket, for one of the large blast furnaces being built there at that time It was particularly desired to get a smooth seam, so that the cooling water would stay on the jacket, better than was possible for a film of water to do on such a surface when broken by seams and rivets, and also to have only one thickness of metal, to eliminate the great liability of burning, due to double thickness.

The bosh jacket was in the form of a truncated cone, and was eleven feet in diameter at the bottom, sixteen feet at the top, nine feet high, and made of half inch stock throughout

In fabricating this job it was built in four sections or segments and welded along the vertical joints, with an oxy-acetylene torch. When the welds were finished the joints were ground smooth and were hardly perceptible. The job was eminently satisfactory and in several years of continuous service, has shown no indication of weakening at the welded joints

Welding Pieces of Different Thickness —Oxy-acetylene welding is not easily applied to pieces of different thickness, because the melting of the two edges is not equal, and does not take place at the same time Since the torch is too powerful for the thin piece or too weak for the thick piece. A clever welder, however, can manage his torch so that the heat given to the two edges is proportional to their thickness, but if the difference is very great, the joint is not easily obtained

Effects of Expansion:—The effects of expansion often act in such manner that the edges to be poined separate and approach each other alternately. If one wishes to join two plates by autogenous welding, and the edges have been arranged parallel, when the weld has commenced one first observes a widening of the space, at the other end of the plate. See figure 53. If the welding is continued, the deviation quickly stops and the opposite movement takes place, that is, the edges approach, and as the weld advances they will overlap each other. See figure 54.

Fig. 66.

FABRICATING A BOSH JACKET IN SHOPS AT DULUTH, MINN.

Fig. 52   Fig. 53   Fig. 54

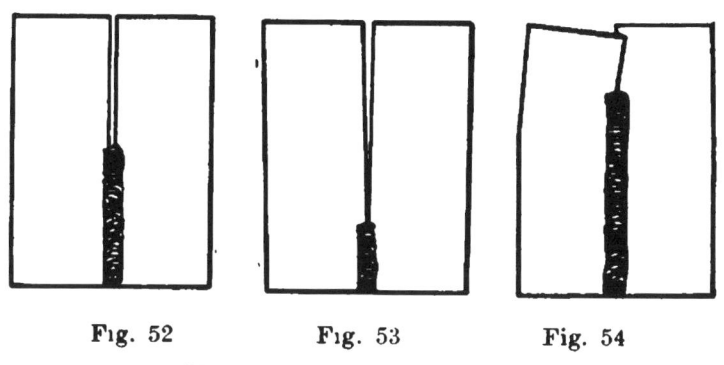

EXAMPLES OF EXPANSION

To overcome this final overlaping, two methods may be followed: one is to separate the edges before commencing to weld, as shown in figure 55, and the other to weld in spots about a foot apart, throughout the length of the joint. This latter method is called tacking.

In the first case the initial separation should be about 1-20 of the length of the weld, and as the weld progresses the space at the far end may be allowed to close a small amount, thus continue closing the space as the weld advances, at a ratio that will bring the edges together when the weld reaches the end. In starting this job the edges will first be placed parallel until a few inches are welded and then they will be sprung open, as suggested.

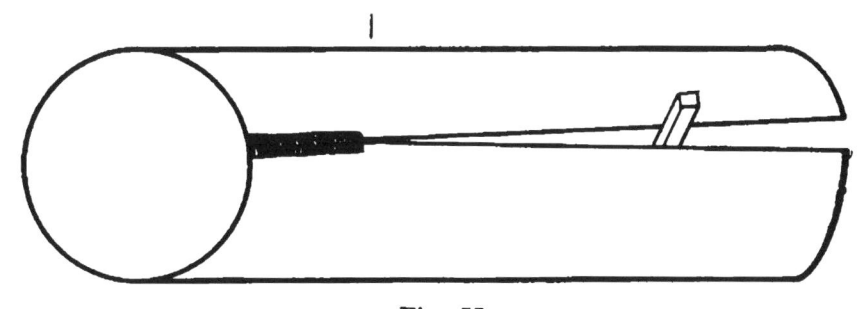

Fig 55

METHOD OF OVERCOMING EFFECTS OF EXPANSION, WHILE WELDING PARALLEL EDGES

If the system of tacking is used, the expansion cannot act laterally, as in the previous case, and this causes a deformation as shown in figure 56 In the majority of cases, it is easy to bring the plates back to the original position.

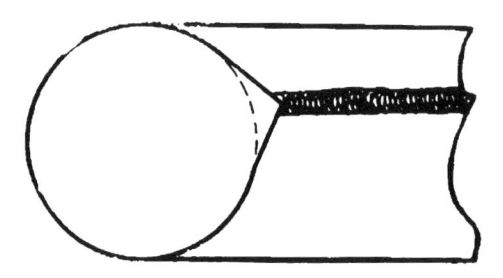

Fig 56

DEFORMATION CAUSED BY EXPANSION WHEN THE JOINT HAS BEEN PREVIOUSLY TACKED

The Preparation of Joints—Welding very thin pieces, is especially difficult on account of the great liability of melting holes through the material. In this kind of work, the method of overlapping the edges as shown in figure 57 is very faulty. The best method being to bend the edges up as shown in figure 58 These upturned edges are melted down and furnish welding material.

If the plates are thick enough to permit beveling they may be prepared as in figures 59 and 60 This is explained quite thoroughly under "General Notes on Welding."

In Joining plates at right angles, the groove for welding is obtained without beveling, by simply arranging as shown in figure 62.

The joint in figure 61, which is not beveled at all, is bad when the plates are over $1/8$ of an inch thick, because the amount of penetration is doubtful. The arrangement shown in figure 63 is favorable from the view point of penetration, but the weld is difficult to make and in figure 64 the difference in thickness between the beveled side and the unbeveled side, makes the job difficult for the reason that the heavy part requires more heat than the other, but the joint can be successfully made by skillful manipulation

Fig. 57

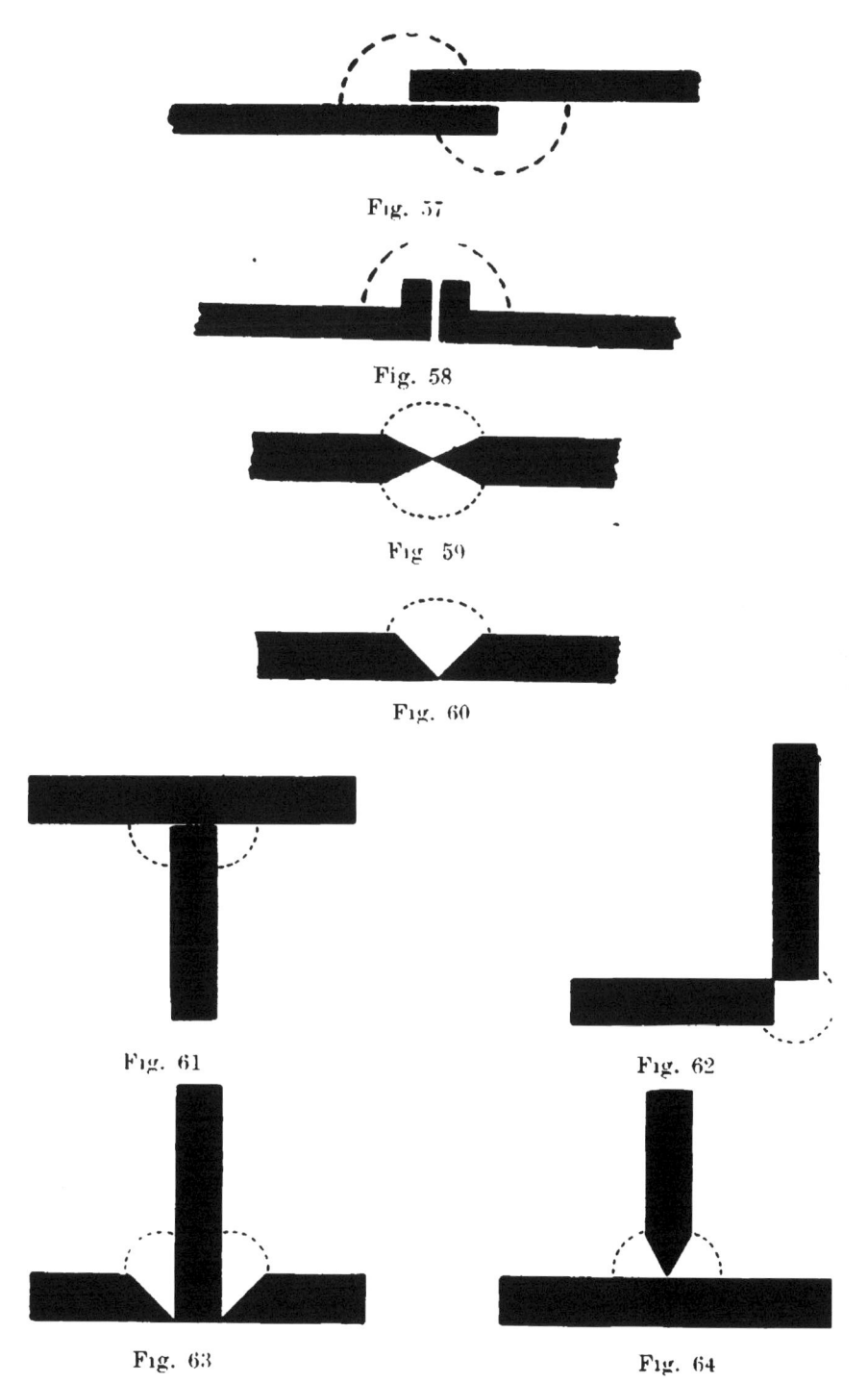

Fig. 58

Fig. 59

Fig. 60

Fig. 61   Fig. 62

Fig. 63   Fig. 64

GOOD AND BAD EXAMPLES OF PREPARED JOINTS

Welding a Crack in a Boiler Sheet:—It is very exasperating and sometimes embarrassing to the welder, to nicely finish a weld in a cracked plate, and then stand back and see it reopen and grow a few inches longer, when the sheet cools off. This is sure to happen unless some provision is made to take care of the expansion.

A careful study of this phenomenon will be of benefit, and when the principle is understood it will help to solve other difficulties which will occur in boiler work.

When the metal around the crack is brought to a welding heat, it becomes soft and incapable of resisting compression, consequently, the expansion caused by the heat, pushes the soft metal together, so that when it cools off it *would* be shorter than it was before; but to shorten is impossible, because it is a part of a cold, solid, uncompromising plate. The tension thus caused by the shrinkage is enormous.

If the weld was strong enough to hold, it would produce strains in the rest of the boiler and would be objectionable.

To successfully weld a crack of this kind, it is only necessary to relieve the sheet of the strains resulting from shrinkage, and this may be done by preheating an extensive portion of the plate, at each end of the fracture, and keep it hot during the whole performance of welding.

Preheating in this way will cause the fracture to open and when the welder can clearly see the opening, he can apply his process to the weld and finish as in welding any other plate. Then when the whole area cools it will resume its normal position and be void of strains or the liability to crack.

After reading the preceding pages of this book, the welder should not need cautioning, to be sure and weld deep through to the other side of the plate.

Welding in a Patch:—In welding in a patch, the effects of expansion and contraction can be overcome without preheating. This is done by "dishing" the patch.

Cut the patch a little bigger than the hole and then "dish" it until the outside edges just fill the opening After beveling the edges of the hole and patch, it is inserted in the opening with the convex side out, and tacked in several places to secure it. Finish the weld as instructed in previous paragraphs and when shrinkage ensues, the convex patch is flattened down with a hammer. Flattening the patch enlarges it and compensates for the shrinkage.

Welding Flues:—The oxy-acetylene torch can be used very successful for re-tipping flues. By the old method flues and tips were scarfed, brought to a welding heat in the blacksmith forge and then welded by means of hammer blows. To do this work properly it would therefore require the services of an experienced blacksmith and in comparison to the new method takes considerable longer. Flues can best be re-tipped by means of the oxy-acetylene torch by first grinding the ends of the flue and tip to a bevel edge, butting the beveled ends together and welding them in place. Care must be taken not to allow the metal to flow through and leave a rough edge on the inside. Should this occur, the end of the flue could be slipped over a piece of round shafting to be used as a mandrel, and hammered smooth. Very little extra metal should be added on the outside otherwise the flue would not pass through the flue sheet.

Where a comparatively pure supply of water is available, it has been found practicable to weld the flues directly to the flue sheets. When they are so welded, it is of course difficult to take them out and hence this method is not recommended where it is necessary to frequently remove the flues.

In welding new flues to the flue sheet, they should be welded on one end only, the other end being rolled. The welding should be done first leaving the other end free to take care of the expansion and contraction. The flue should be allowed to extend through the flue sheet about one-eighth inch or three-sixteenths inch and then welded around between the end of the flue and the sheet.

CHAPTER XIV.

CARBON BURNING.

Carbon is a fuel. It is the carbon in coal that burns and gives us heat by chemically uniting with oxygen to form carbon dioxide as explained on page 17. Soot is carbon which has been liberated by heat, and for lack of oxygen was not consumed If soot can be heated in the presence of oxygen it will burn and leave no ashes, but if the oxygen is derived from the air this is difficult to accomplish because the predominance of nitrogen, in the air, absorbs the heat of reaction, lowering the temperature below the point at which the carbon will burn. When pure oxygen is used, the burden of nitrogen is avoided and the carbon will burn rapidly.

Soot or carbon frequently accumulates in the compression chamber of internal combustion engines, to such an extent that it interferes with its perfect working.

In the past, it has been the practice of mechanics to remove this carbon by scraping. The operation required considerable time and was quite an expense, but since the advent of cheap oxygen, this carbon is being removed by burning it

The process consists of starting combustion with a little kerosene, which is sprinkled into the cylinder, ignited and immediately followed with a stream of oxygen. The carbon flashes into a flame and as long as it is fed with oxygen it burns to the last trace.

By this method a four cylinder motor can be cleaned in twenty minutes, at a very trifling expense.

Directions for a Carbon Burner—Have the piston at the top of the compression stroke, and remove the spark plug and valve cap. Then sprinkle about half a tablespoon of kerosene into the valve chamber, and cylinder head. After is has soaked into the carbon, light it and immediately insert the long slender nozzle of the torch. When the oxygen comes in contact with the carbon it will burst into flames and during the earlier part of the process, these flames will rush from all the openings. For this reason it is advisable to keep the face away from the work

CARBON BURNING

When the carbon diminishes the flame will be replaced by sparks and the flow of gas should be increased, to make it hunt all the little corners. This may be assisted by thrusting the torch around into different parts.

If the flame goes out suddenly, put in more kerosene and relight it. This may have to be repeated several times. After the cylinder is cleaned, blow all the loose particles out with compressed air.

Cleaning cylinders in this way does not heat them to as high a temperature as they attain in service.

Fig. 65
CARBON BURNER AT WORK

Table X.

COST OF CUTTING WITH THE OXYGEN JET.

Thickness of plate in inches	Cost of gases		Total cost of gases	Cost for labor		Total Cost of cut per foot
	Oxygen @ 2c per ft.	Acetylene @ 7/8c per ft.		Time per foot in seconds	Amount @ 40c per hour	
¼	$0.0082	$0.0022	$0.01	24	$0.0026	$0.0126
½	0.0154	0.0029	0.018	30	0.0033	0.0213
1	0.0244	0.0036	0.028	38	0.0042	0.0322
1½	0.0306	0.0057	0.036	46	0.005	0.041

Table XI

COST OF WELDING WITH THE OXY-ACETYLENE TORCH

Thickness of plate in inches	Cost of gases		Total cost of gases	Cost for labor		Total Cost of Weld per foot
	Oxygen @ 2c per ft.	Acetylene @ 7/8c per ft.		Time per foot in minutes	Amount @ 40c per hour	
⅛	$0.012	$0.011	$0.023	3.33	$.022	$0.045
¼	0.065	0.056	0.121	8.57	.056	0.177
⅜	0.19	0.16	0.35	15.	.10	0.45
½	0.30	0.259	0.56	20.	.13	0.69
⅝	0.55	0.49	1.04	30.	.20	1.24

TABLE XII

QUANTITY OF GAS IN CYLINDERS

Under Varying Pressures and Constant Temperatures
Rated capacity and pressure of drum at 68° Fahrenheit

100 Cubic Feet at 300 Lbs Pressure		100 Cubic Feet at 1800 Lbs Pressure		200 Cubic Feet at 1800 Lbs Pressure	
Varying Pressures	Quantity in Cu Ft	Varying Pressures	Quantity in Cu Ft	Varying Pressures	Quantity in Cu Ft
300	100	1800	100	1800	200
270	90	1620	90	1620	180
240	80	1440	80	1440	160
210	70	1260	70	1260	140
180	60	1080	60	1080	120
150	50	900	50	900	100
120	40	700	39	700	78
100	33	500	28	500	56
75	25	300	17	300	33
50	17	100	6	100	11
25	8	18	1	18	2
3	1	9	½	9	1

TABLE XIII

VARIATION OF PRESSURE IN CYLINDERS

Under Varying Temperatures and Constant Quantity

Temperature Fahrenheit	Initial Pressure at 68° F		
	100 Lbs	300 Lbs	1800 Lbs
120	109 85	329 5	1973
100	106 05	318 2	1909
80	102 3	306 8	1841
60	98 48	295 5	1773
40	95 7	284 1	1705
20	90 91	272 7	1636
0	87 12	261 4	1568
−10	85 23	255 7	1534
−20	83 33	250 0	1500

TABLE XIV

COMPARISON OF DEGREES CENTIGRADE AND FAHRENHEIT.

Below Zero C — F	Above Zero C — F	Above Zero C — F	Equivalents C — F
200 — 328	525 — 977	1250 — 2282	1 — 1 8
150 — 238	550 — 1022	1275 — 2327	2 — 3 6
100 — 148	575 — 1067	1300 — 2372	3 — 5 4
50 — 58	600 — 1112	1325 — 2417	4 — 7 2
	625 — 1157	1350 — 2462	5 — 9 0
Above Zero C — F	650 — 1202	1375 — 2507	6 — 10 8
	675 — 1247	1400 — 2552	7 — 12 6
0 — 32	700 — 1292	1425 — 2597	8 — 14 4
25 — 77	725 — 1337	1450 — 2642	9 — 16 2
50 — 122	750 — 1382	1475 — 2687	10 — 18 0
75 — 167	775 — 1427	1500 — 2732	11 — 19 8
100 — 212	800 — 1472	1525 — 2777	12 — 21 6
125 — 257	825 — 1517	1550 — 2822	13 — 23 4
150 — 302	850 — 1562	1575 — 2867	14 — 25 2
175 — 347	875 — 1627	1600 — 2912	15 — 27 0
200 — 392	900 — 1652	1625 — 2957	16 — 28 8
225 — 437	925 — 1697	1650 — 3002	17 — 30 6
250 — 482	950 — 1742	1675 — 3047	18 — 32 4
275 — 527	1000 — 1832	1700 — 3092	19 — 34 2
300 — 572	1025 — 1877	1725 — 3137	20 — 36 0
325 — 617	1050 — 1922	1750 — 3182	21 — 37 8
350 — 662	1075 — 1967	1775 — 3227	22 — 39 6
375 — 707	1100 — 2012	1800 — 3272	23 — 41 4
400 — 752	1125 — 2057	1825 — 3317	24 — 43 2
425 — 797	1150 — 2102	1850 — 3362	25 — 45 0
450 — 842	1175 — 2147	1875 — 3407	
475 — 887	1200 — 2192	1900 — 3452	
500 — 932	1225 — 2237	2000 — 3632	

TABLE XV

WEIGHT OF OXYGEN GAS DRUMS

Oxygen	Capacity	Pressure	Weight
Low Pressure	100 cub ft	300 lbs	150 lbs
High Pressure	100 cub ft	1800 lbs	125 lbs
High Pressure	200 cub ft	1800 lbs	150 lbs

TABLE NO. XVI

CONSUMPTION OF GASES AND COST OF OXY-ACETYLENE WELDING

APPROXIMATE

Tip.	Acetylene Pressure	Oxygen Pressure	Thickness of Metal	Acetylene Con-sumption.	Oxygen Con-sumption.	Lineal Ft Per Hour	Total Cost With Labor at 30c Per Hour	Cost Per Lineal Ft Including Labor at 30c Per Hour.
1	1	$1\frac{1}{4}$	$\frac{1}{32}$	3 ft	3 02	60	0 384	0064
2	$1\frac{1}{8}$	$1\frac{1}{2}$	$\frac{3}{32}$	4 62	4 62	40	0 4288	0107
3	$1\frac{1}{4}$	$1\frac{3}{4}$	$\frac{1}{16}$	7 51	7 56	25	0 5112	02
4	$1\frac{1}{2}$	2	$\frac{1}{8}$	11 42	11 51	18	0 62236	0345
5	$1\frac{1}{2}$	$2\frac{1}{4}$	$\frac{3}{16}$	16 10	16 42	10	0 7572	0757
6	2	$4\frac{1}{4}$	$\frac{1}{4}$	23 01	23 38	7	0 95168	1319
7	$2\frac{1}{2}$	$7\frac{3}{4}$	$\frac{5}{16}$	30 12	31	5	1 1609	232
8	3	10	$\frac{3}{8}$	39 12	40 08	4	1 4145	3536
9	4	$15\frac{1}{2}$	$\frac{1}{2}$	46 12	46 36	3	1 76	88
10	$4\frac{3}{4}$	25	$\frac{3}{4}$ & $\frac{5}{8}$	55 40	56 45	2	2 32	116
11	$9\frac{1}{2}$	45	Heavy	78 20	80 15			
12	12	54	Extra Heavy	102 12	105 20			

INDEX

A

Atomic theory	13
Atomic weights	12
Acetylene	23
Alloys	41
Alloys—table of	42
Aluminum	43
Acetylene generators	44
Assembling cutting torch	56
Automatic Oxygen regulator	59
Acetylene Regulator	58
Acetylene—oxygen required to consume	50
Acetylene in drums	81
Acetone	81
Adjusting the flame	95
Aluminum welding	105
Air—oxygen from	19

B

Building in gear teeth	4
Boyles Law	25
British thermal unit	31
Blister Process	39
Brass	40
Brass—welding	104
Building a furnace	76
Beveling	89
Bronze—welding	104
Boiler making	118

C

Comparative cost of cutting	7
Chemistry	11
Origin	11
Elements	11
Symbols	11
Atomic weights	12
Notation	12
Affinity	13
Atomic theory	13
Valence	14
Re-action	16
Combustion	16
Flame	16

C

Calcium Carbide	21
Calorie	31
Centigrade	32
Coefficients of expansion	33
Calculations in expansion	33
Conductivity of heat	34
Cast iron	35
Cast iron welding	101
Cast iron flux	88
Copper	39
Copper flux	88
Copper welding	104
Carbide	21
Carbide to water generator	45
Carbide—yield of gas	
Composition of sludge	72
Cost of acetylene	69
Clean oxygen hose	80
Cleaning the weld	89
Charges for welding service	84
Chloride of potash method of producing oxygen	18
Cutting torch	53
Cutting iron and steel	110
Cutting steel floor beams	115
Cutting machines	113
Cost of gas for cutting	114
Carbon burning	126

D

Drip type generator	45
Dissolved acetylene	81
Defects of welds	100
Directions for carbon burning	126
Drums of acetylene	81

E

Examples of savings	4
Elements	11
Electrolysis	19
Effect of temperature on pressure	28
Expansion	32

INDEX

E

Expansion—coefficients of	33
Expansion—calculating the	33
Expansion—precautions regarding	91
Expansion—effects of	92-120-121
Economy of preheating	94
Examples in welding	107

F

Flame	16
Fahrenheit	31
Ferrous group of metals	35
Flashing Back	50-80
Fluxes	87
For cast iron	88
For copper	88
Filling in holes	99
Fabricating a bosh jacket	119

G

Gas—	
Oxygen	17
Hydrogen	20
Nitrogen	21
Acetylene	23
Gas—weight of	21
Gas—quantity in drums	26
Gas—yield from carbide	23
Gay Lusac's Law	27
General notes on welding	89

H

Hydrogen	20
High pressure pump	29
Heat	30
Heat conductivity	34
Heat liberated by carbide in water	44
High pressure torch	52
How and where to preheat	95
Handling the torch	96
Holes—filling in	99

L

Low pressure torch	51
Loss of pressure in pipes	70
Loss of pressure in valves and fittings	71
Leaks in oxygen pipes	73
Lead burning	106
Leaks—testing for	73
Lead welding	106
Liquid air—oxygen from	19

M

Metals and their properties	35
Malleable cast iron	36
Malleable cast iron welding	102
Melting temperatures	39
Movements of the torch	98
Machine for cutting	113
Manganese dioxide method of producing oxygen	18

N

Nitrogen	21
Neutral flame	95

O

Oxygen	17
From air	19
By electrolysis	19
From chloride of potash and manganese-dioxide	18
Oxyacetylene cutting	6
Oxyacetylene torch	50
Oxygen required to consume acetylene	5
Operating plants	68

P

Phases of combustion	17
Physics	25
Phneumatics	25
Pressure regulators	58

INDEX

P

Preheating furnaces	76
Protecting apparatus	77
Portable acetylene drum plant	81
Portable acetylene generator plant	83
Preheating to eliminate defects	94
Preheating how and where	95
Puddle-system	105
Preparing the joint	122
Propagation of flame	50

R

Repairing locomotive cylinder	2-3
Repairing pump case	10
Reaction	16

S

Steel	38
Steel welding	101
Selecting a generator	47
Sludge—composition of	72
Scrapping a boiler	116

T

Time required to cut plates	7
Temperature	31
Thermometers	31
Temperature of melting	39
Thermite	43
Typical carbide to water generator	45
Torches	50
Torches—for machines	57
Testing pipe lines	73
Time card for welding shop	86
Theory of cutting	110

U

Use of the oxyacetylene torch	4
Using the cutting torch	111
Unit of heat	31
Unit—British thermal	31

V

Valence	14
Velocity of propagation of flame	50
Vulcan automatic acetylene generator	61
Vulcan portable generator plant	67

W

Welding crank shaft	8-107
Weight of gases	21
Wrought iron	37
Welding—	
Iron and steel	101
Cast iron	101
Malleable cast iron	102
Copper	104
Brass	104
Bronze	104
Aluminum	105
Lead	106
Welding rods and fluxes	87
Welding table	74
Welding—examples in	107
Auto cylinders	108
Auto springs	109
Crack in boiler	124
Patch in boiler	124
Flues in boiler	125
Welding pieces of different thickness	119

Y

Yield of gas from carbide	23

BIBLIOLIFE

Old Books Deserve a New Life
www.bibliolife.com

Did you know that you can get most of our titles in our trademark **EasyScript**™ print format? **EasyScript**™ provides readers with a larger than average typeface, for a reading experience that's easier on the eyes.

Did you know that we have an ever-growing collection of books in many languages?

Order online:
www.bibliolife.com/store

Or to exclusively browse our **EasyScript**™ collection:
www.bibliogrande.com

At BiblioLife, we aim to make knowledge more accessible by making thousands of titles available to you – quickly and affordably.

Contact us:
BiblioLife
PO Box 21206
Charleston, SC 29413

Printed in Germany by
Amazon Distribution
GmbH, Leipzig